Ready for a life o and adventure as a Florida?

I'm sure you already know...

- Which snakes are venomous?
- How to handle a jellyfish sting?
- The difference between an alligator and a crocodile?
- All about Florida's native sharks and spiders?

NO?!?

What about your pirating skills?

- Can you navigate by the stars?
- Decipher Morse code?
- Read a map, a compass, and tie a knot?
- Know where to find all the best treasure?

NO AGAIN?!?

YOU had better start reading this book!

If yer ready to start your training, write yer pirate name here! □

All rights reserved www.KrakenSky.com

Chapter 1.
Know Yer Critters

Chapter 2.
Know Yer Trade

Chapter 3.
Staying Busy During Life At Sea

Checklist
Check 'em off!

Yer Treasure
Claim it at the back of the book when yer finished!

All rights reserved www.KrakenSky.com

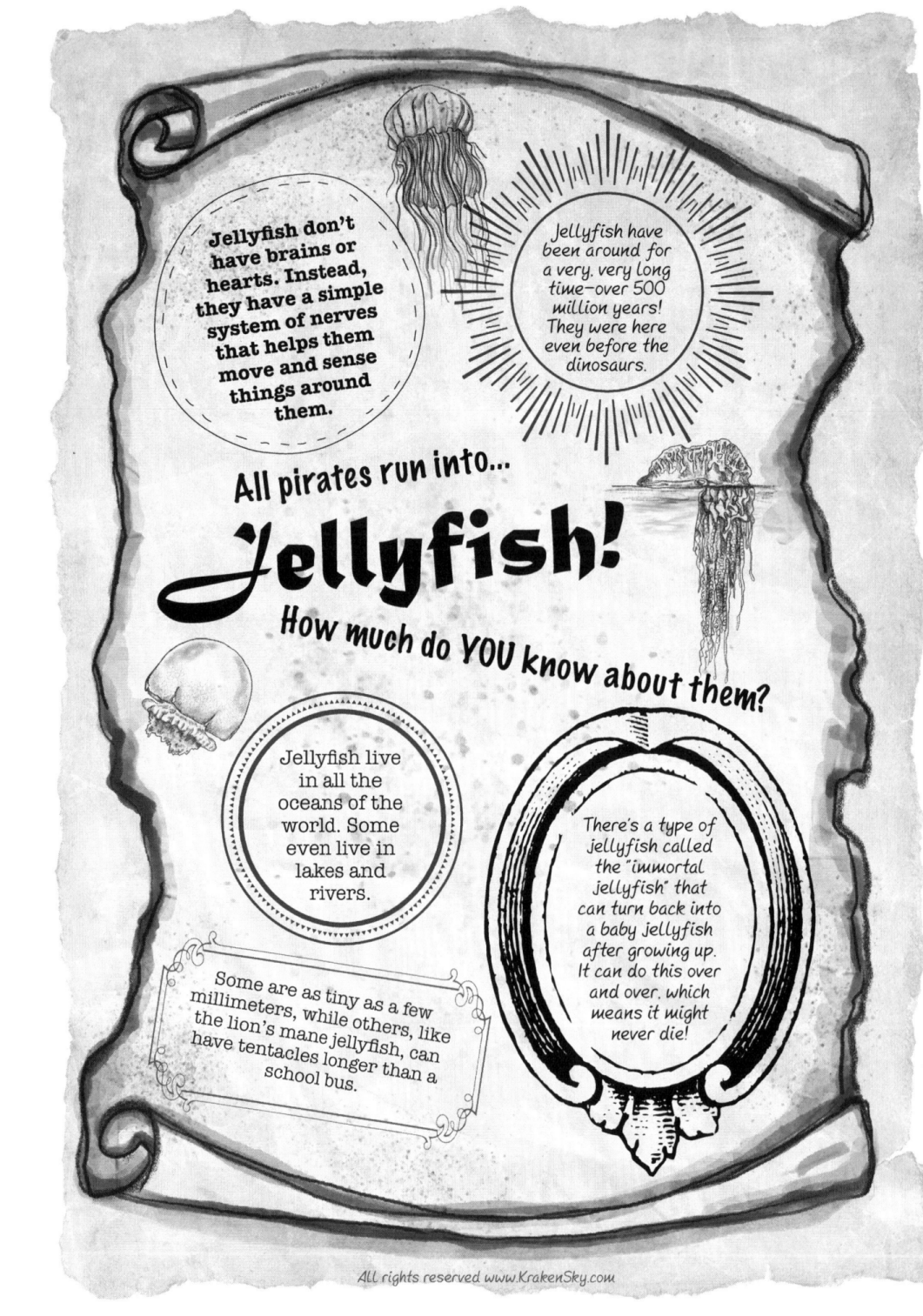

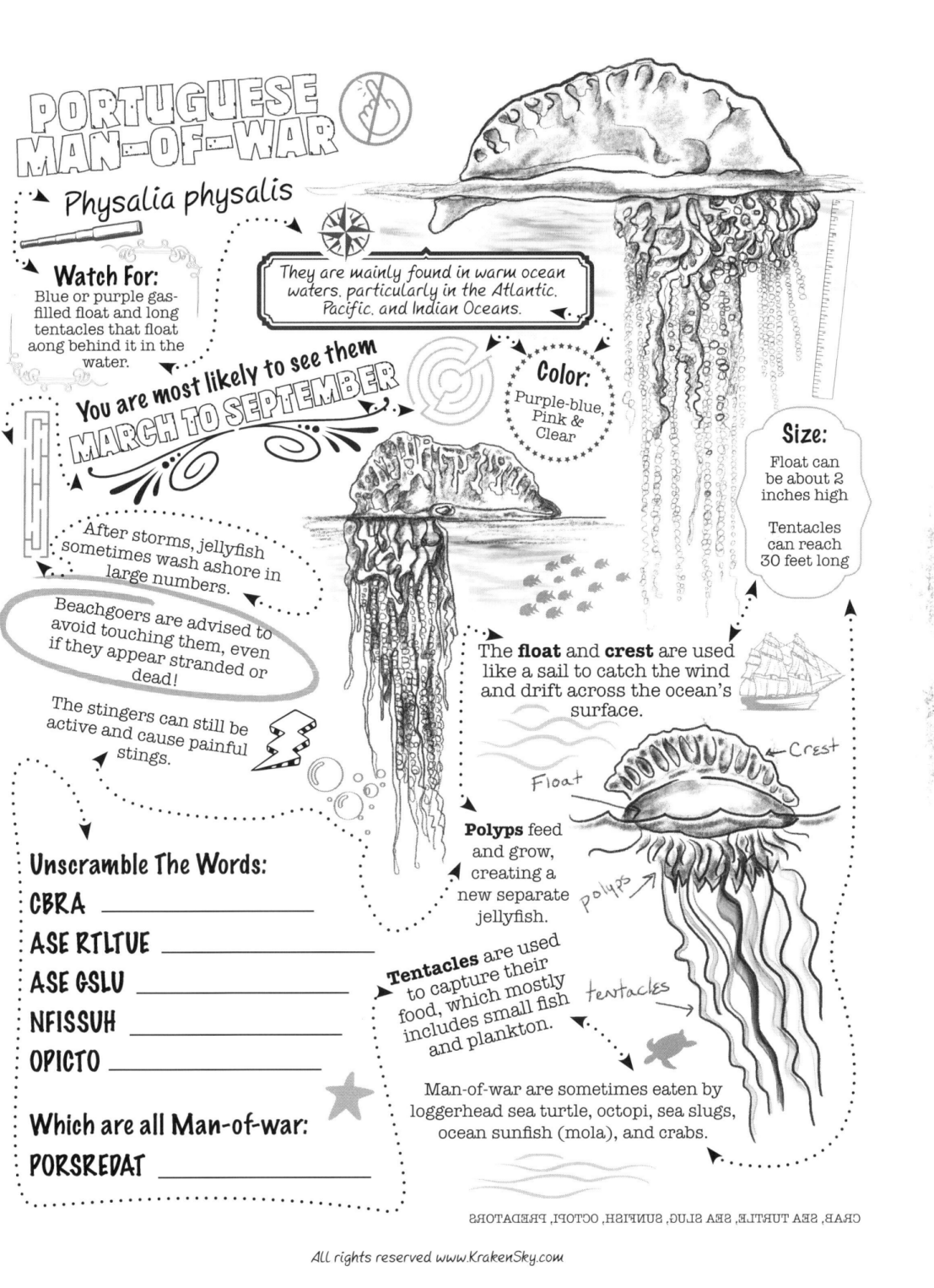

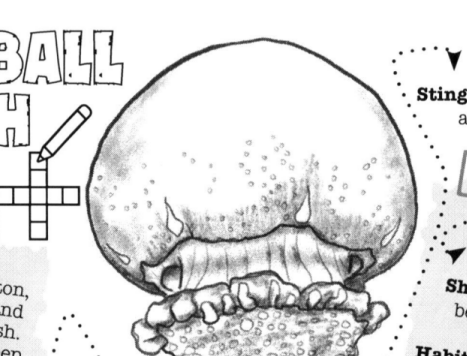

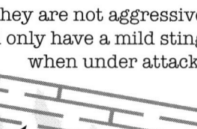
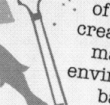

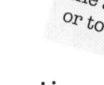
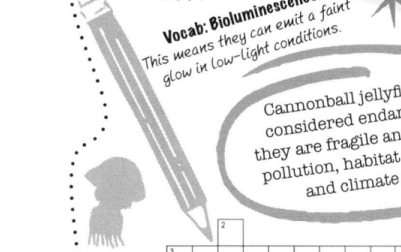
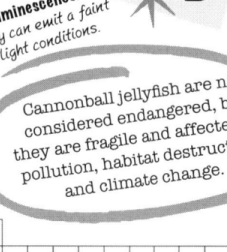

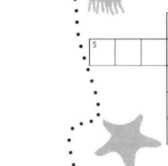

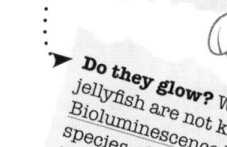

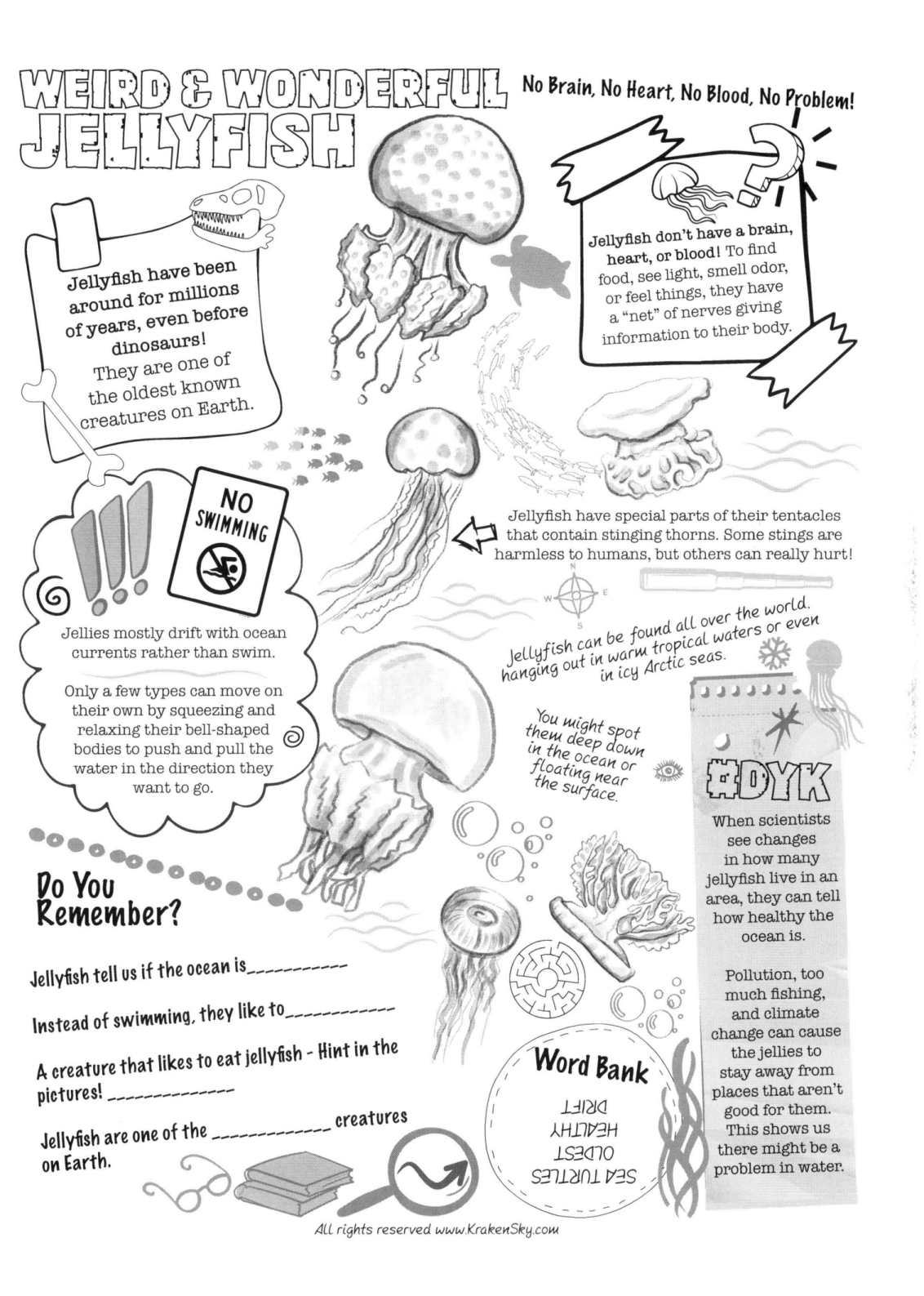

JELLY-FASHION! Bioluminescence

Some jellyfish are like magical glowing creatures! They have a special power called Bioluminescence, which means they can make their own light. They use this power to talk to each other, to find yummy food, and even to scare away scary animals that might want to eat them.

Can you draw a jellyfish?

BIOLUMINESCENCE IS ALSO FOUND IN...

Fireflies: The most well-known bioluminescent insects.

Glow-worms: In addition to fireflies, some other insects, particularly certain species of beetles, are known as glow-worms.

Anglerfish: Deep-sea anglerfish have a bioluminescent lure on their heads that they use to attract prey in the dark depths of the ocean.

Glowing Squid: Some species of squid, like the Hawaiian bobtail squid, have light organs that contain bioluminescent bacteria. The squid use this light to camouflage themselves from predators by matching the moonlight shining through the ocean surface.

All rights reserved www.KrakenSky.com

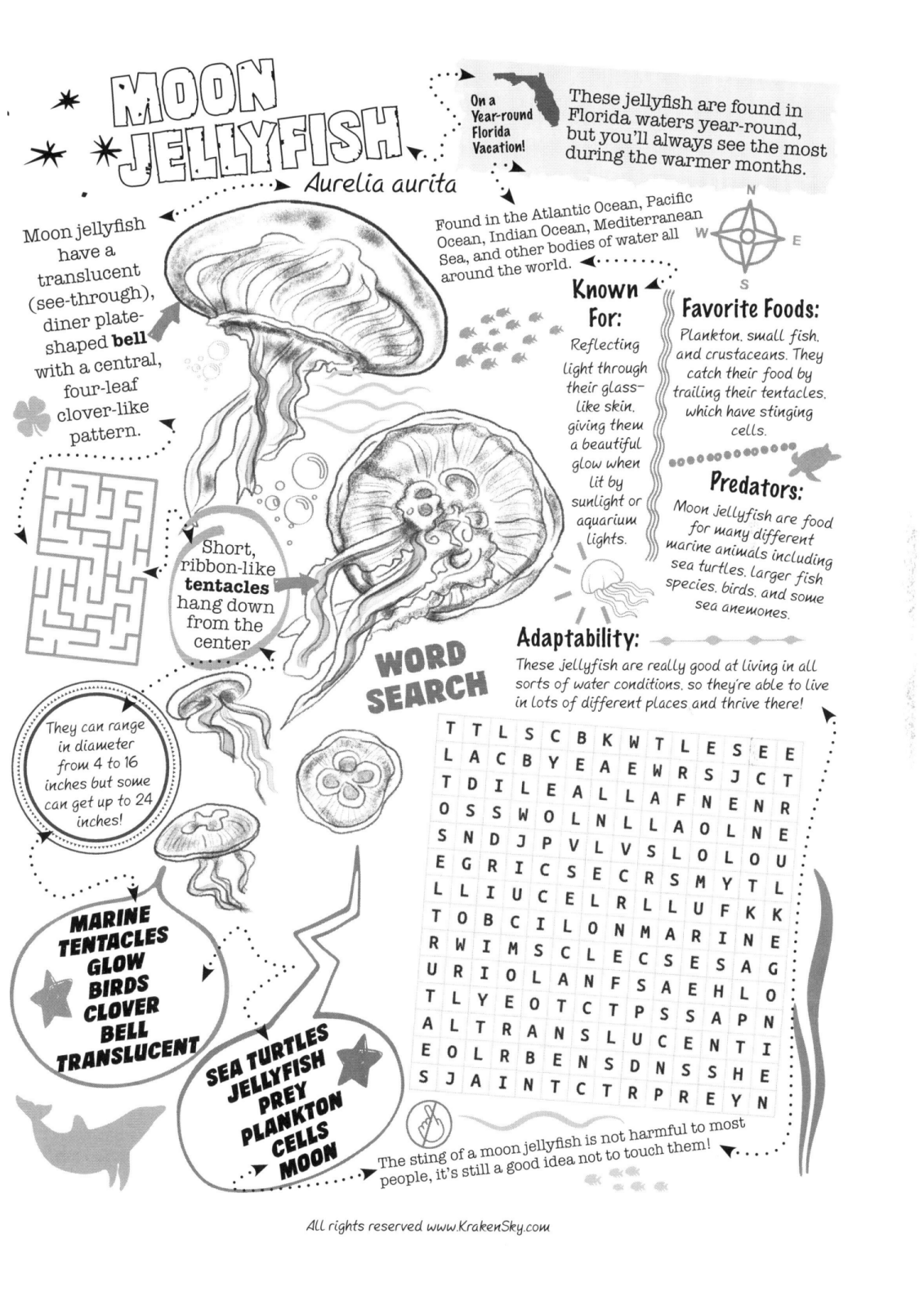

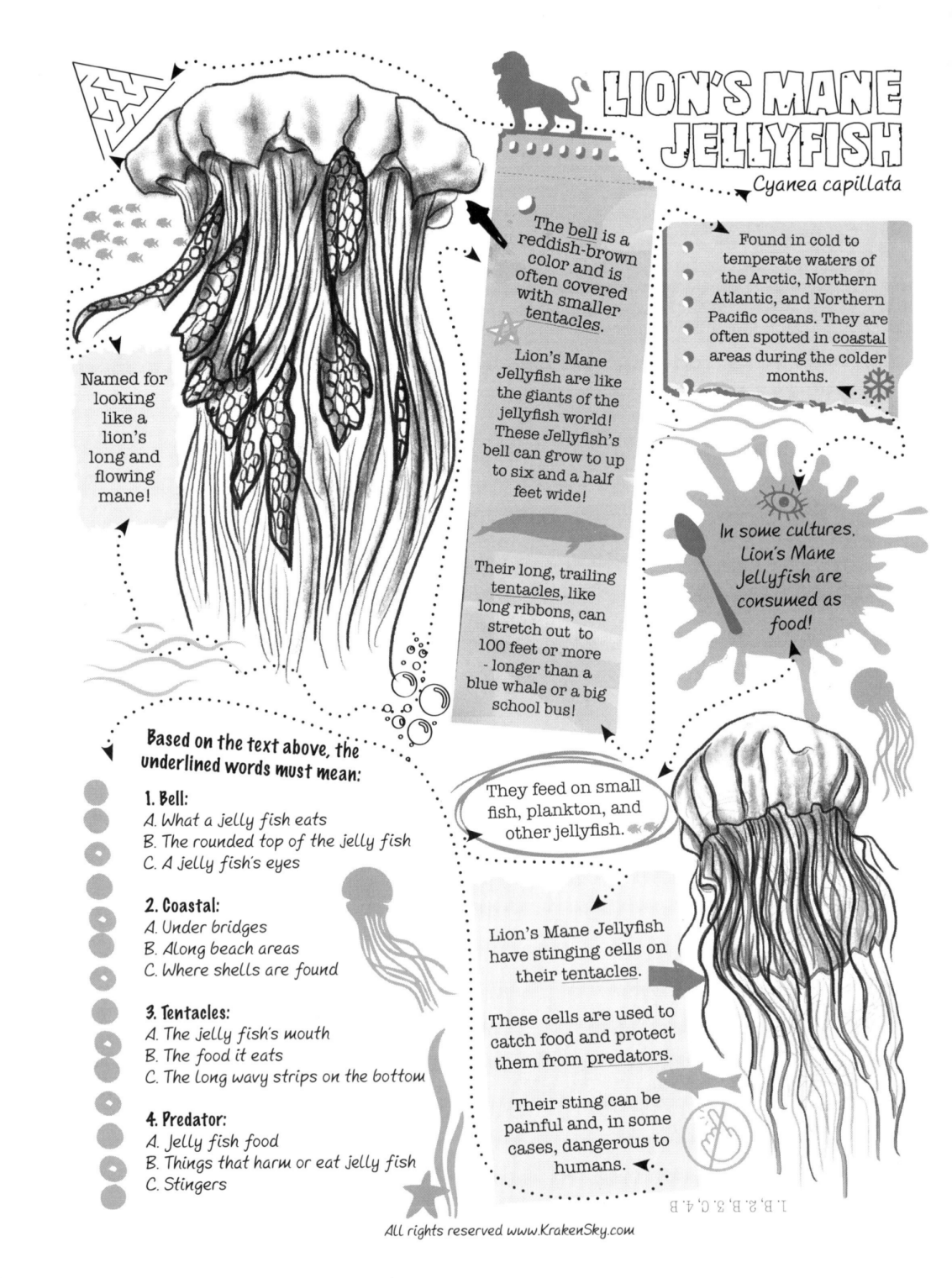

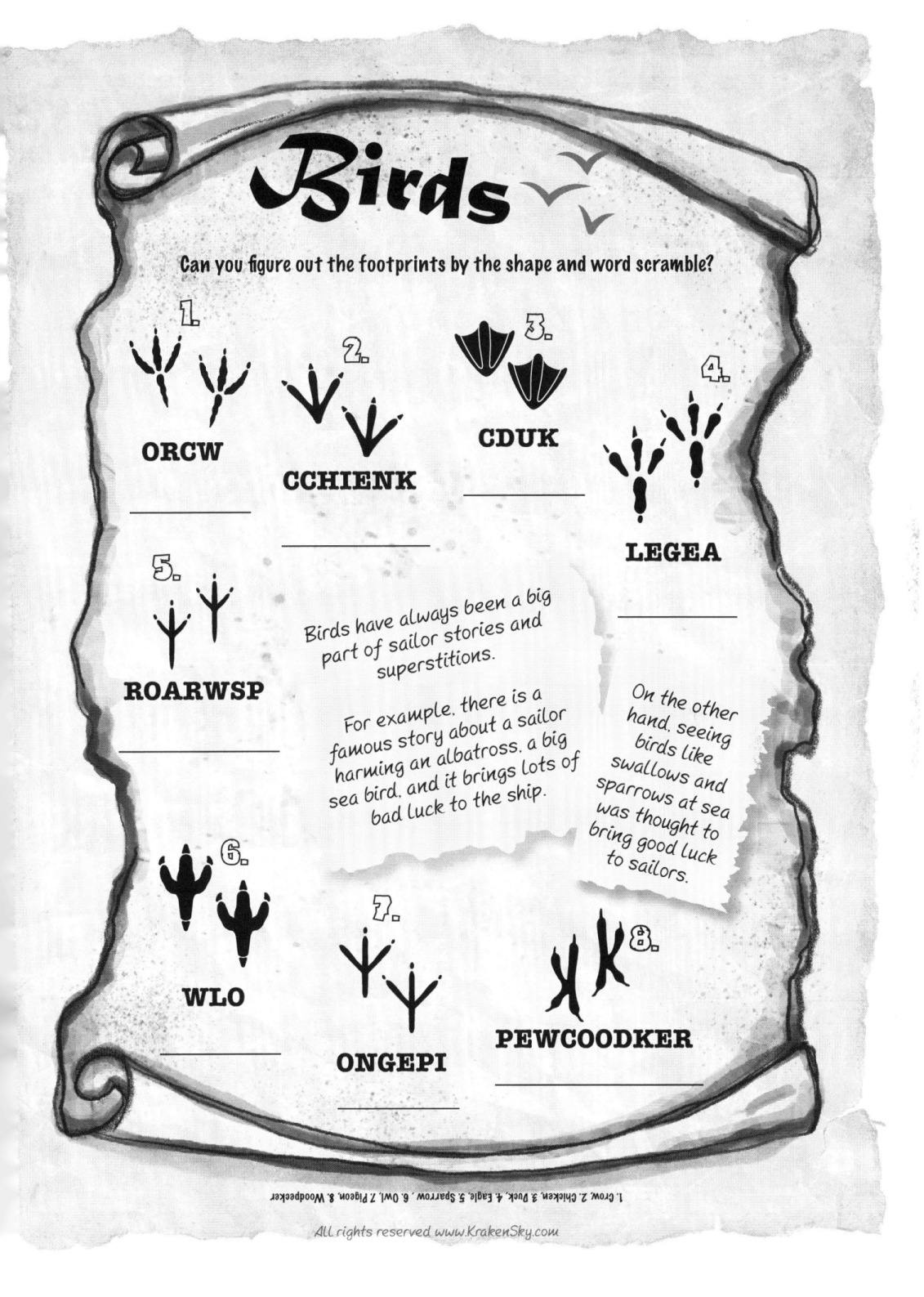

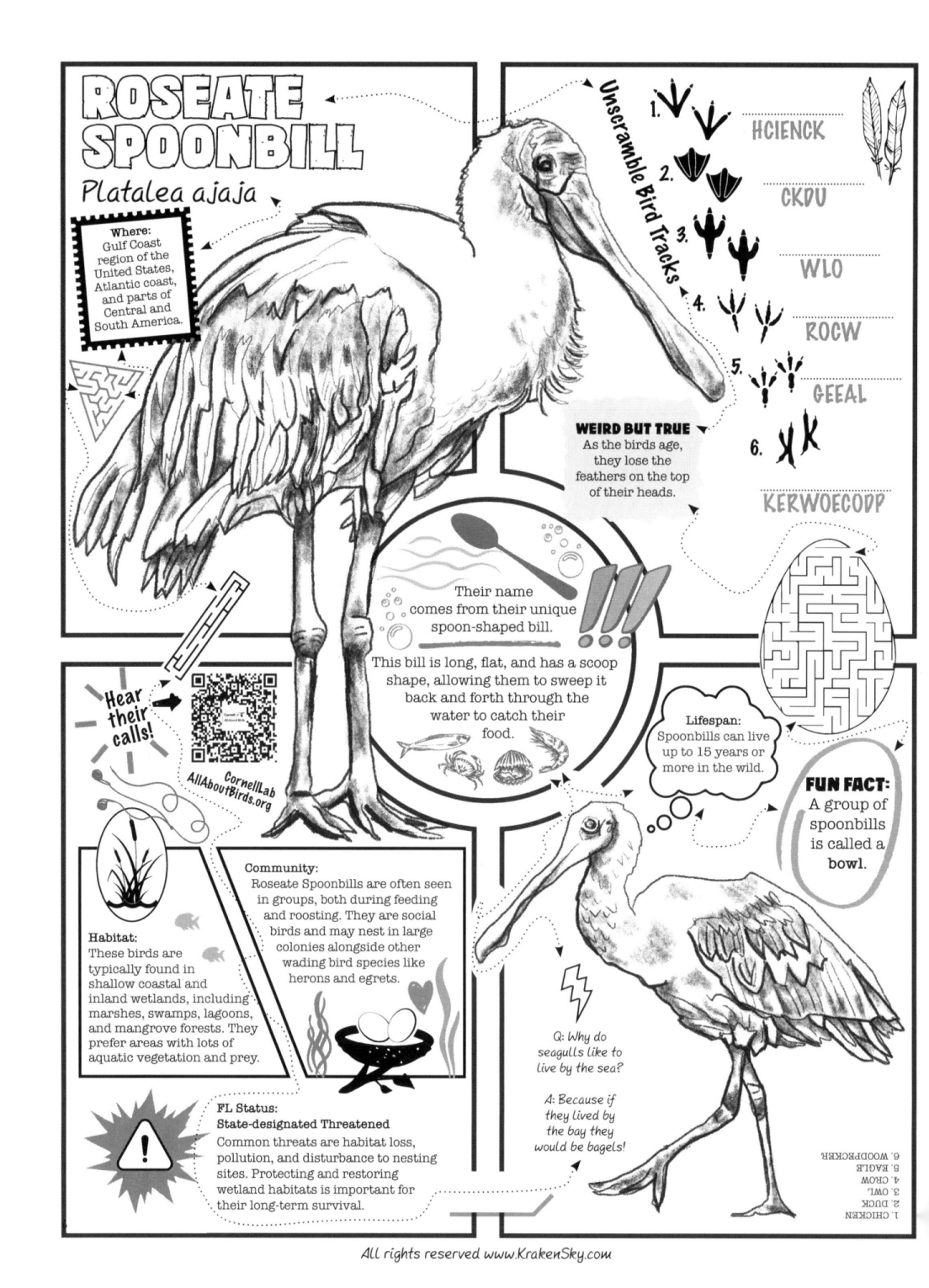

Color: One of the most striking features of the Roseate Spoonbill is its bright pink plumage. This color comes from the crayfish, shrimp, crabs, and small fish they eat.

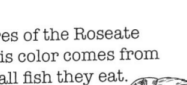

I'm so fancy!

Platalea ajaja

Is the scientific name for...

#DYK:

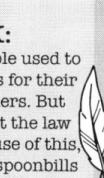

In the past, people used to hunt these birds for their beautiful feathers. But now, it's against the law to do that. Because of this, there are more spoonbills around than before!

Flight Fact:
Roseate Spoonbills are graceful fliers. They often fly in a distinctive V shape and may soar high in the sky during long trips like migration.

ROSEATE SPOONBILL

Length: 30-40 inches
Wingspan: 50-53 inches
Color: Pink wings (with some red on the wings), white neck and back, and pinkish legs and feet.

Crossword

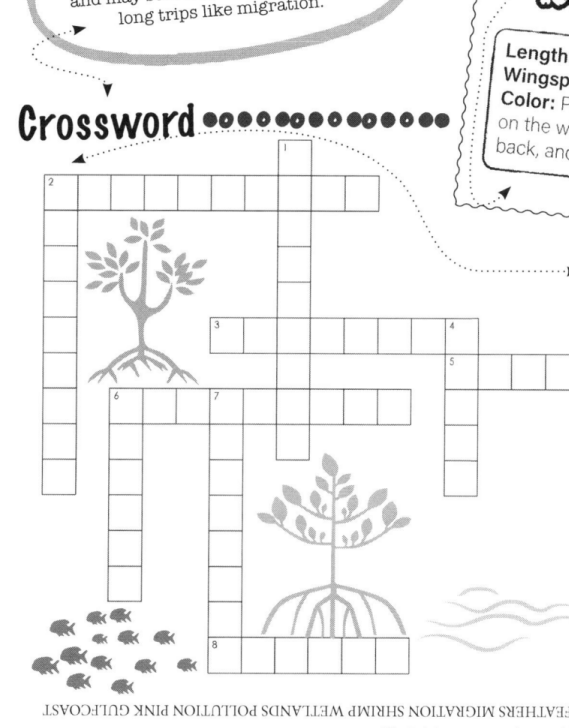

Across:

2. ____ their environment is important
3. The bird's primary habitat
5. Feathers are bright _____
6. One place you can find spoonbills
8. One thing spoonbills eat

Down:

1. They fly in a V shape during _____
2. One threat to their habitat
4. The bird's bill is shaped like a ____
6. Spoonbills often nest and feed in _____
7. They were once hunted for their ____

Word Bank: SPOON GROUPS PROTECTING FEATHERS MIGRATION SHRIMP WETLANDS POLLUTION PINK GULF COAST

All rights reserved www.KrakenSky.com

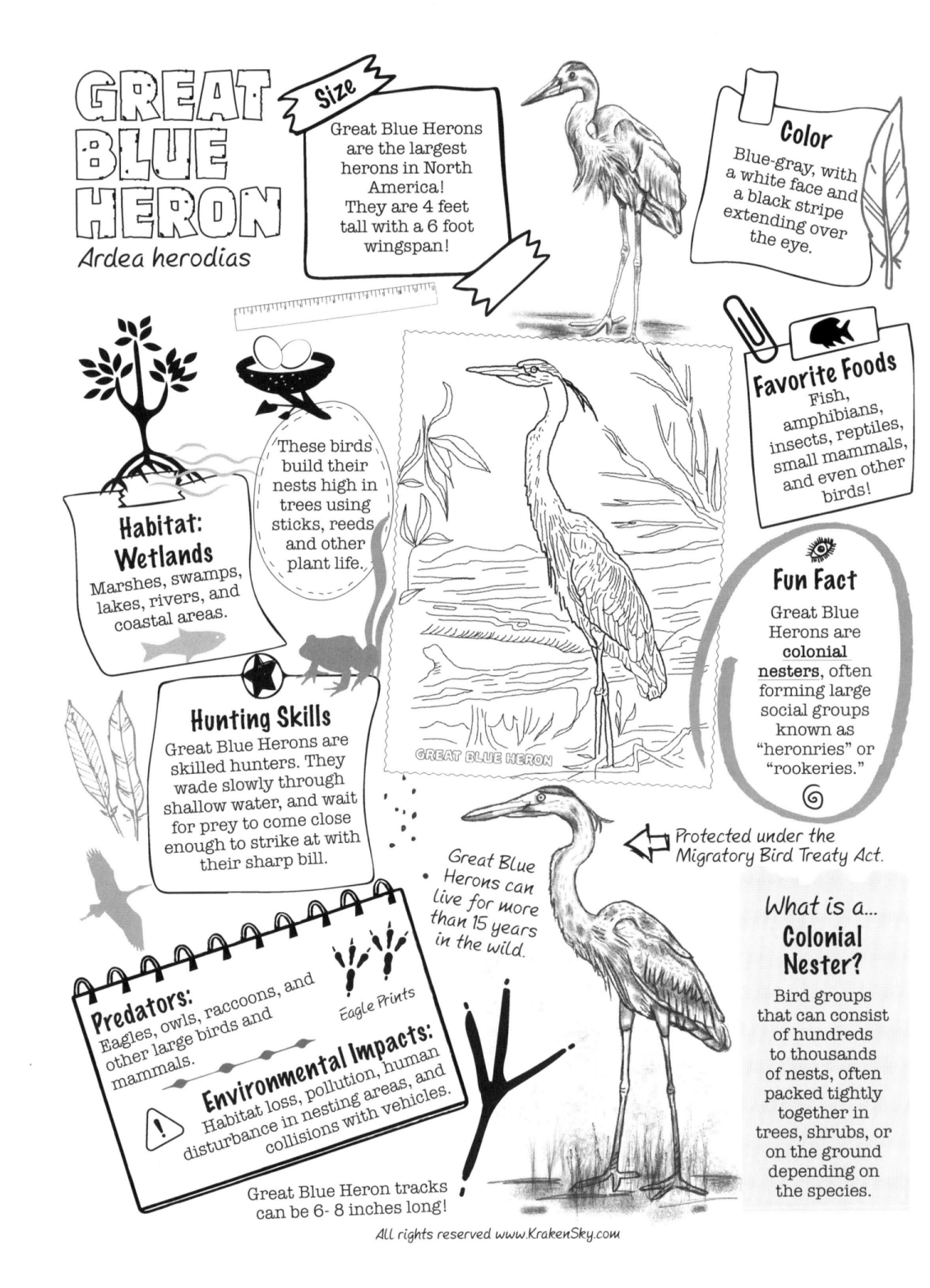

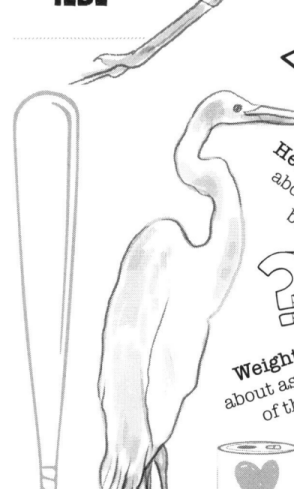

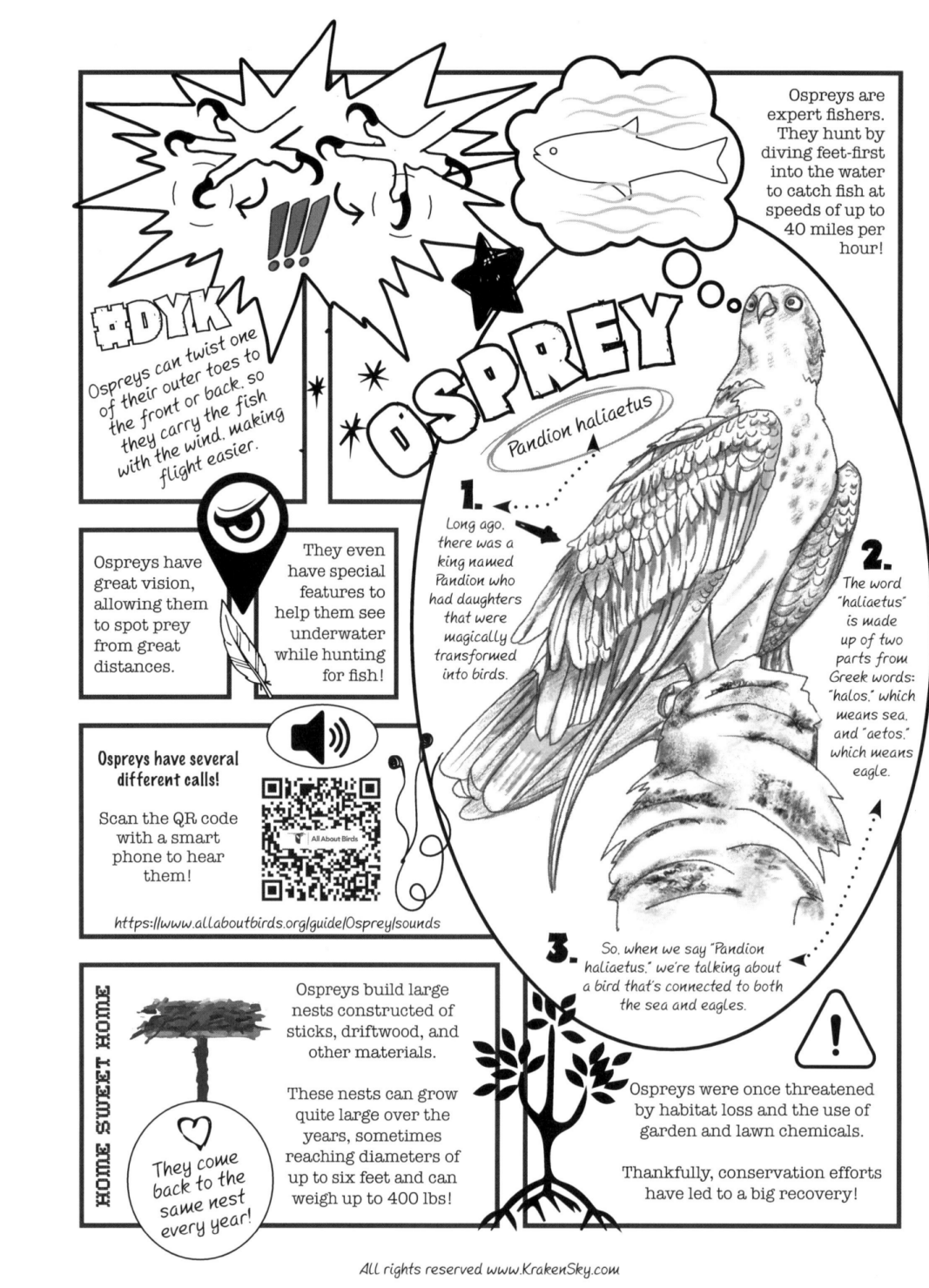

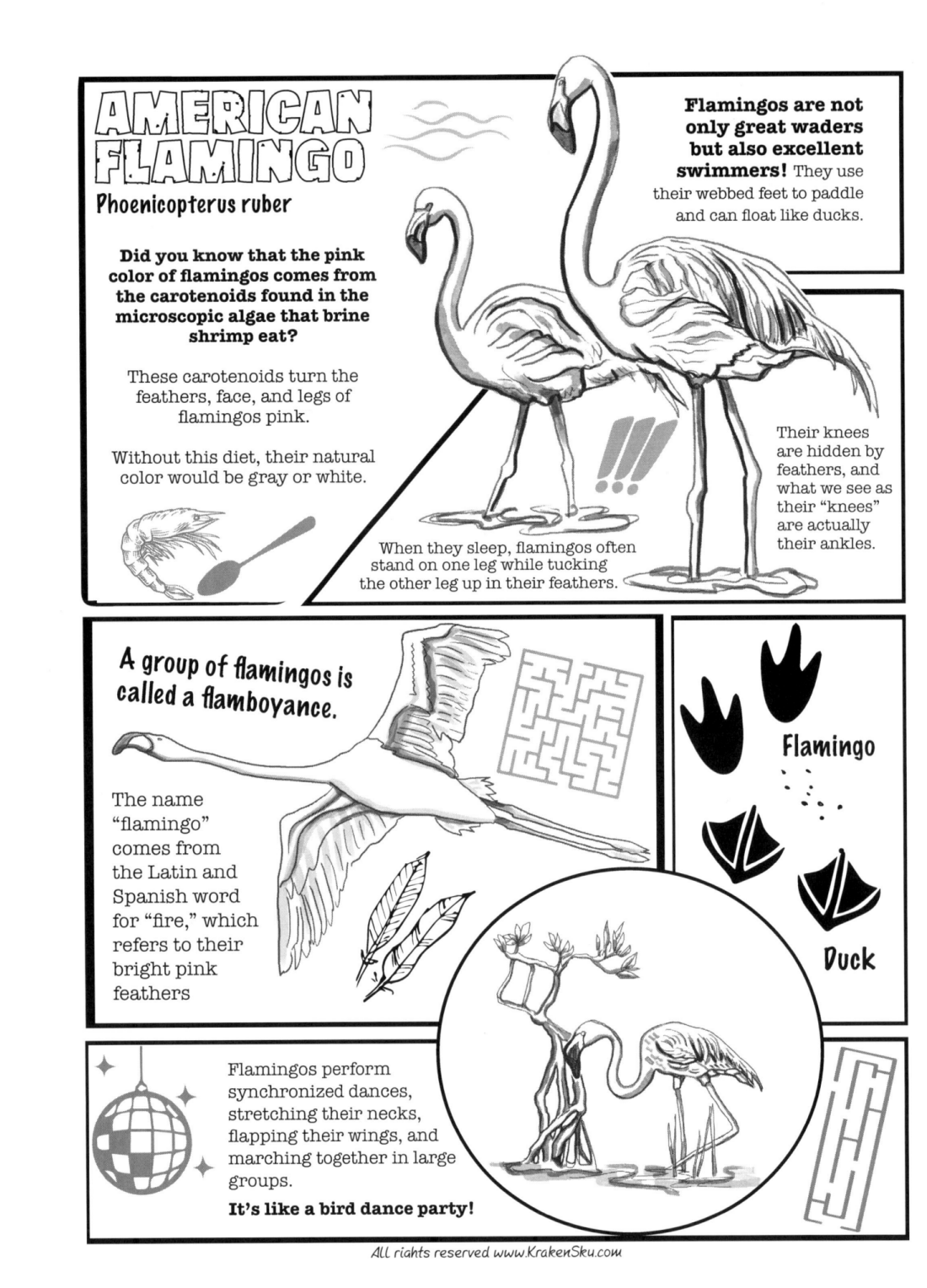

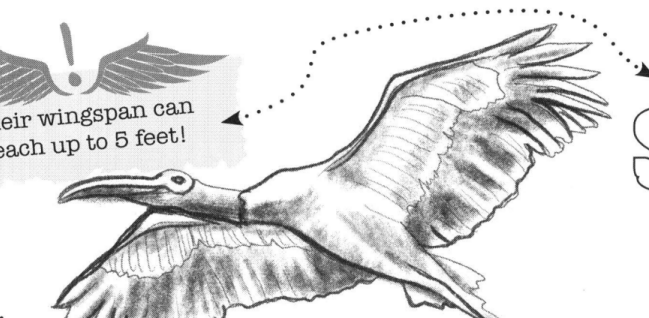

Their wingspan can reach up to 5 feet!

WOOD STORK

Mycteria americana

F I S H B O Q L P W O O D T K
Y I I P A C D V A C K L F J F
J I R T P O G T Q K G H U A R
S D I T Y N M B U Y E Q L V E
T T V U V S U I X F X G D J S
O H E P B E Q L W R Y H M N H
R R R P A R S L R O G C B U W
K E L O F V Q A K G T H Q C A
R A W N K A G S L S G A M S T
P T A D U T D D R T K A W B E
K E D W C I V A E M W U T X R
X N E L N O M A R S H A D R L
G E H M Q N Z V H H N K T U D
K D I S N E B Z X I A K D E M
X J M S R Z V W S L Y T V V R

Wood Storks are entirely white except for their black flight feathers and tail.

WORD SEARCH

RIVER FROGS
LAKE FISH
POND MARSH
SALTWATER WOOD
FRESHWATER STORK
THREATENED BILL
CONSERVATION WADE

Wood storks are large wading birds with a distinct appearance. They have a bald, scaly head, long legs, and a long, thick bill.

33 – 45 INCHES TALL!

Their long legs help them wade through shallow waters in search of a meal.

They are known to move between freshwater and saltwater environments.

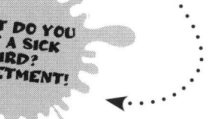

WHAT DO YOU GET A SICK BIRD? TWEETMENT!

All rights reserved www.KrakenSky.com

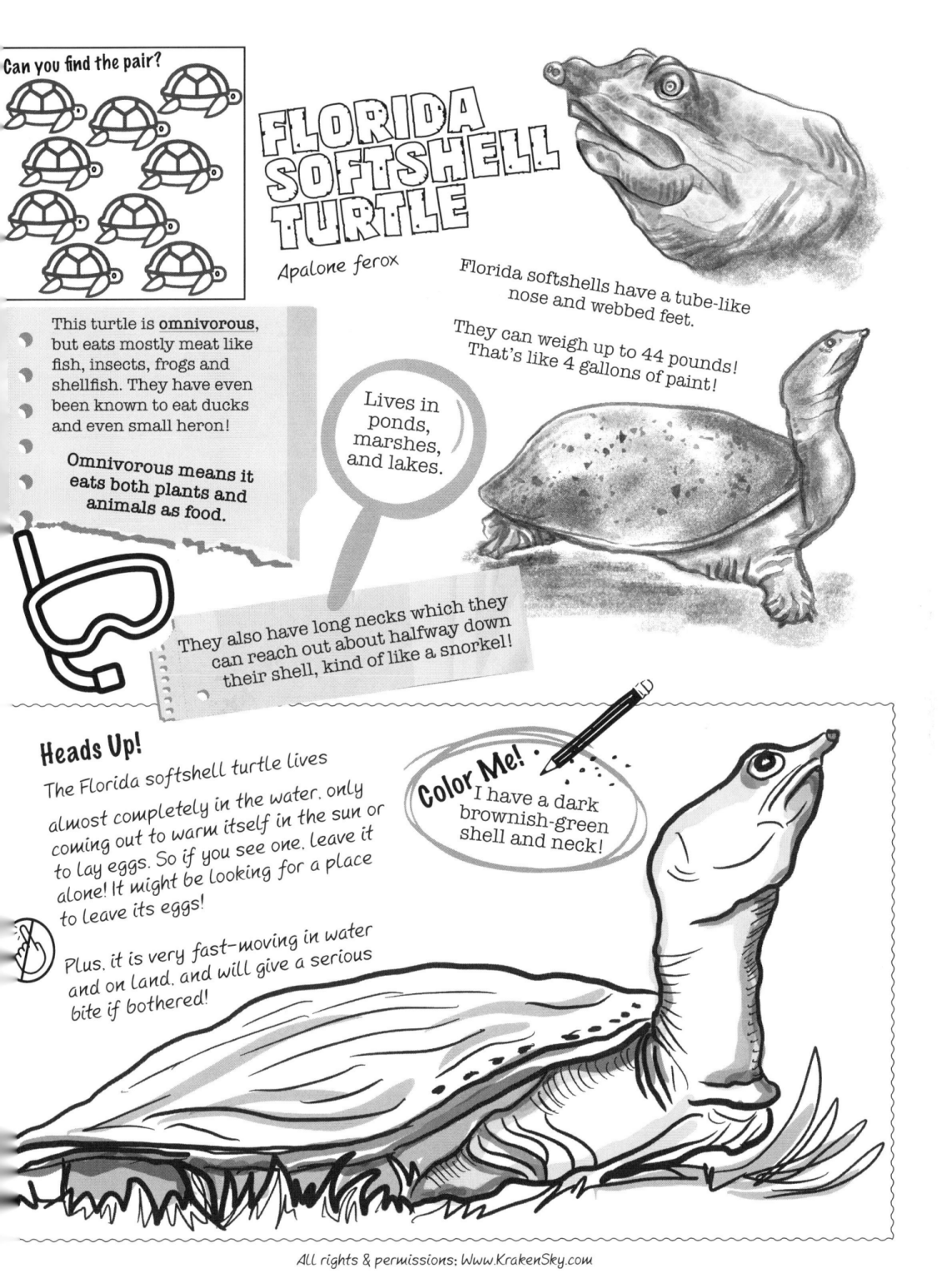

The shortfin mako shark feeds mainly upon cephalopods and bony fish including mackerels, tunas, bonitos, and swordfish, but it may also eat other sharks, porpoises, sea turtles, and seabirds.

They hunt by lunging straight up and tearing off chunks of their preys' flanks and fins. Mako swim below their prey, so they can see what is above and reach prey before it notices them!

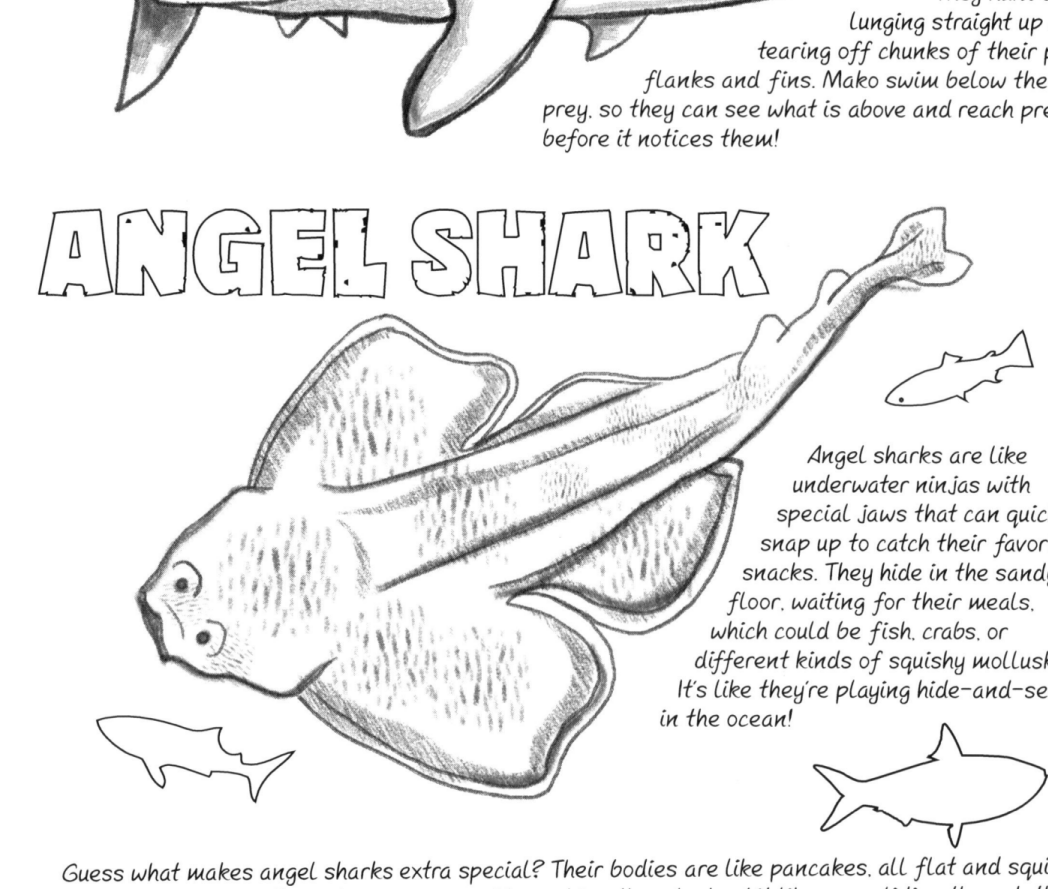

Angel sharks are like underwater ninjas with special jaws that can quickly snap up to catch their favorite snacks. They hide in the sandy floor, waiting for their meals, which could be fish, crabs, or different kinds of squishy mollusks. It's like they're playing hide-and-seek in the ocean!

Guess what makes angel sharks extra special? Their bodies are like pancakes, all flat and squishy! And their fins on the sides are super wide, making them look a bit like rays gliding through the water. It's like they have their own superhero cape fins!

All rights reserved www.KrakenSky.com

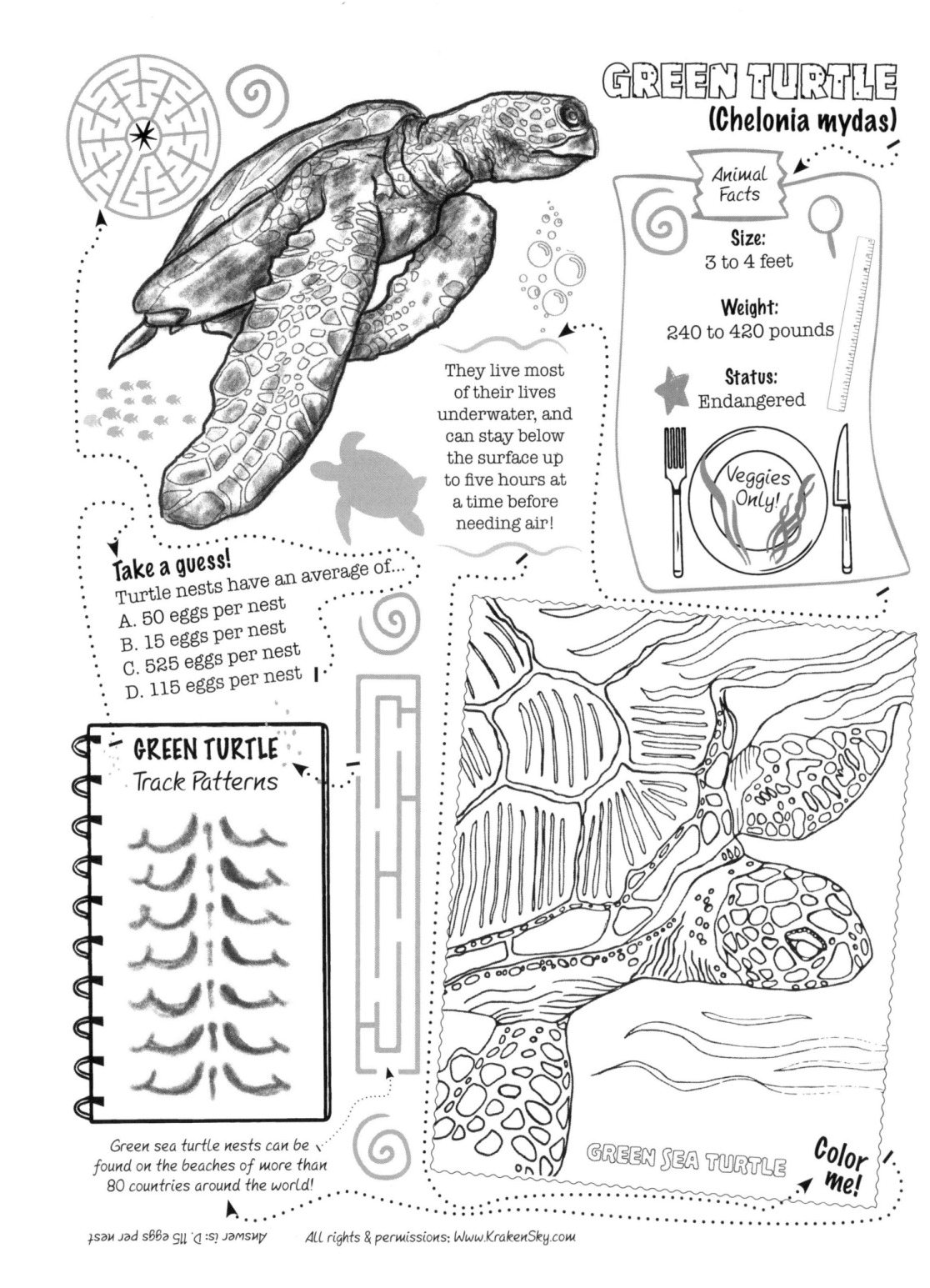

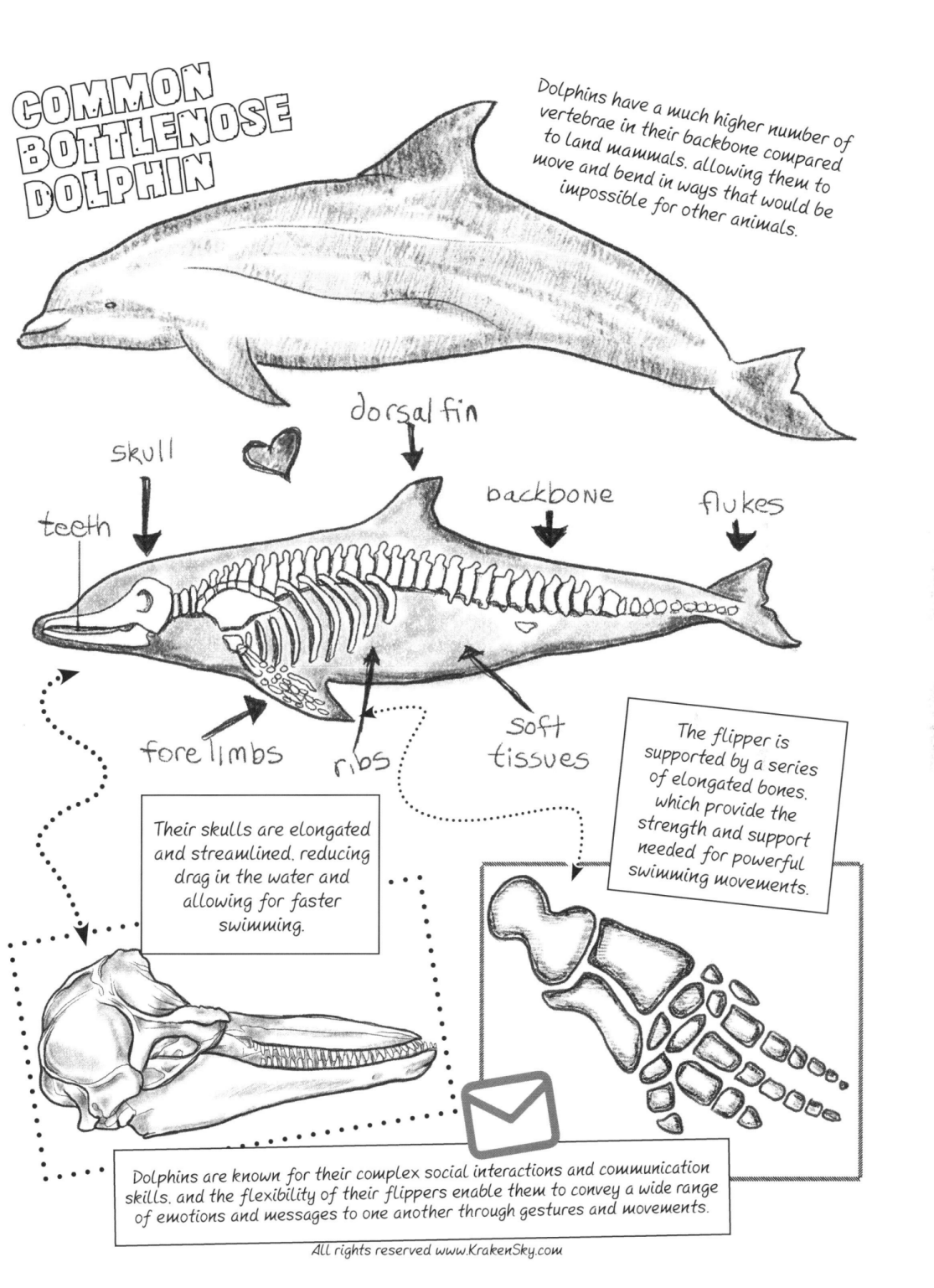

LEMON SHARK

Negaprion brevirostris

Q. How big do Lemon Sharks get?
A. Adult Lemon Sharks can grow up to 10 feet long, making them one of the biggest sharks in the ocean.

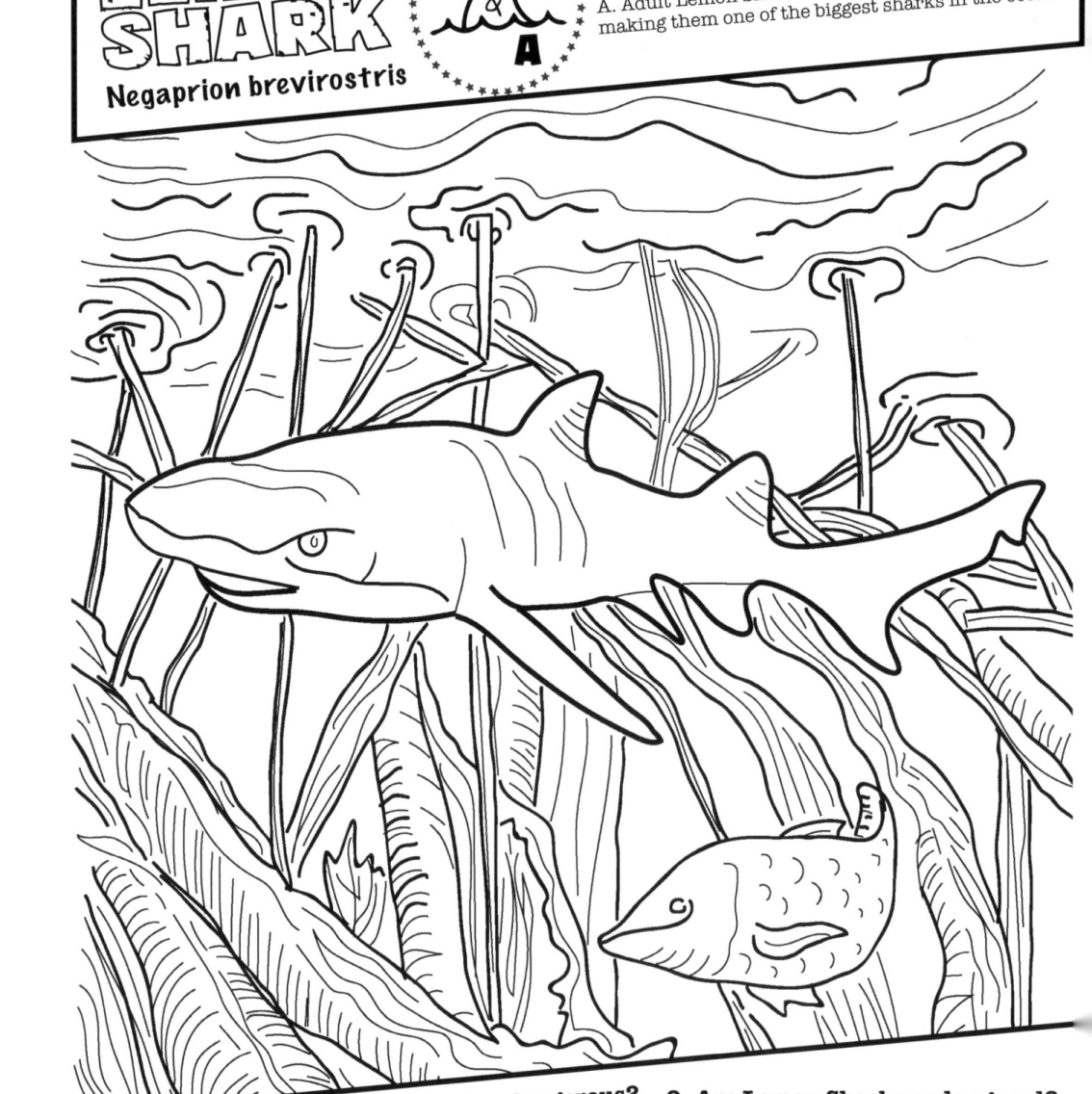

Q. Are they dangerous?
A. While there have been some Lemon Shark attacks on people, they usually don't pose much danger to divers and swimmers.

Q. Why are they called Lemon Sharks?
A. Because of their pale yellow-brownish color.

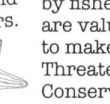

Q. Are Lemon Sharks endangered?
A. Lemon Sharks are sometimes hunted by fishermen because their fins and meat are valuable, and their thick skin is used to make leather. They are listed as Near Threatened by the International Union for Conservation of Nature's Red List.

All rights reserved www.KrakenSky.com

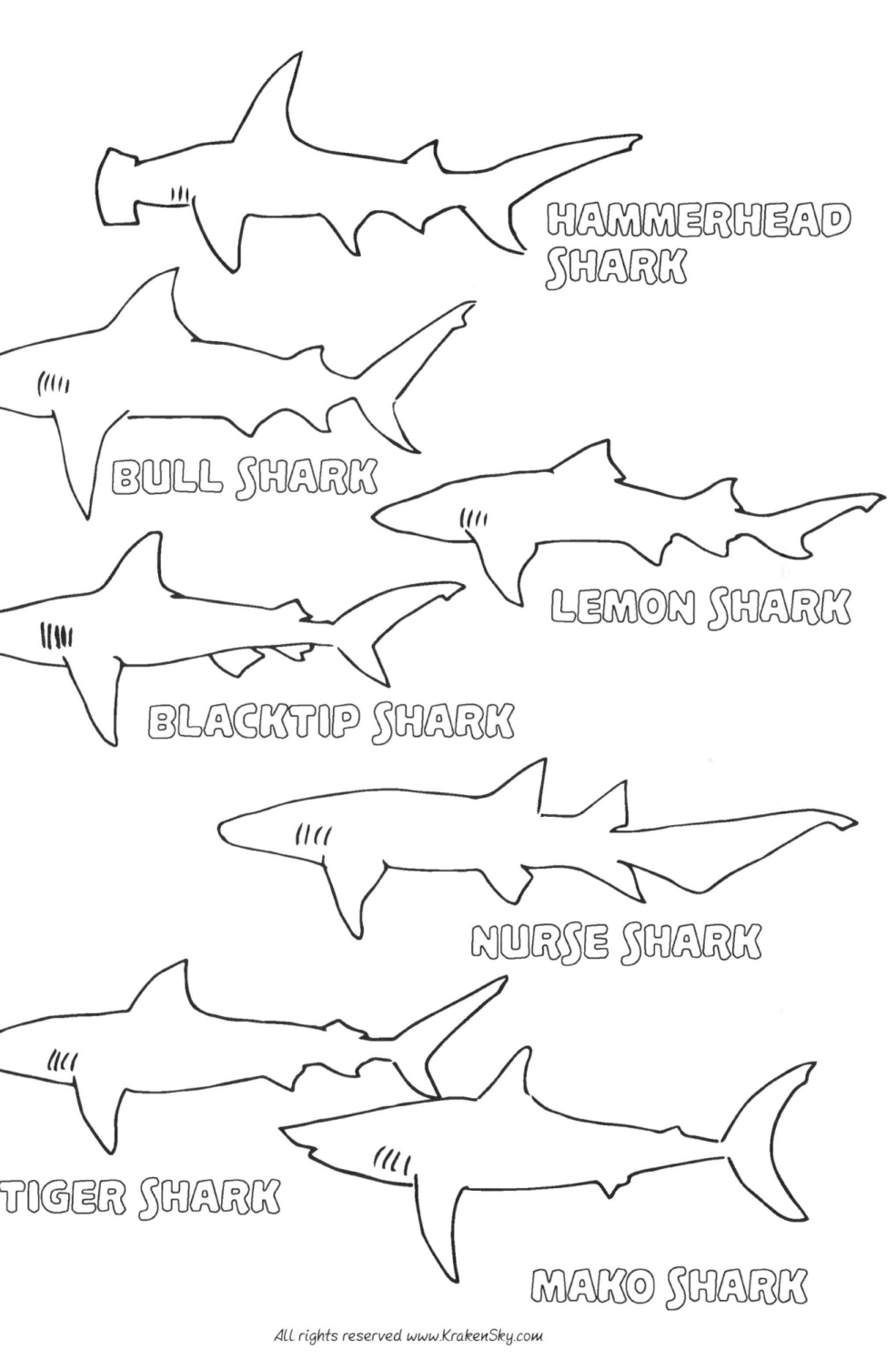

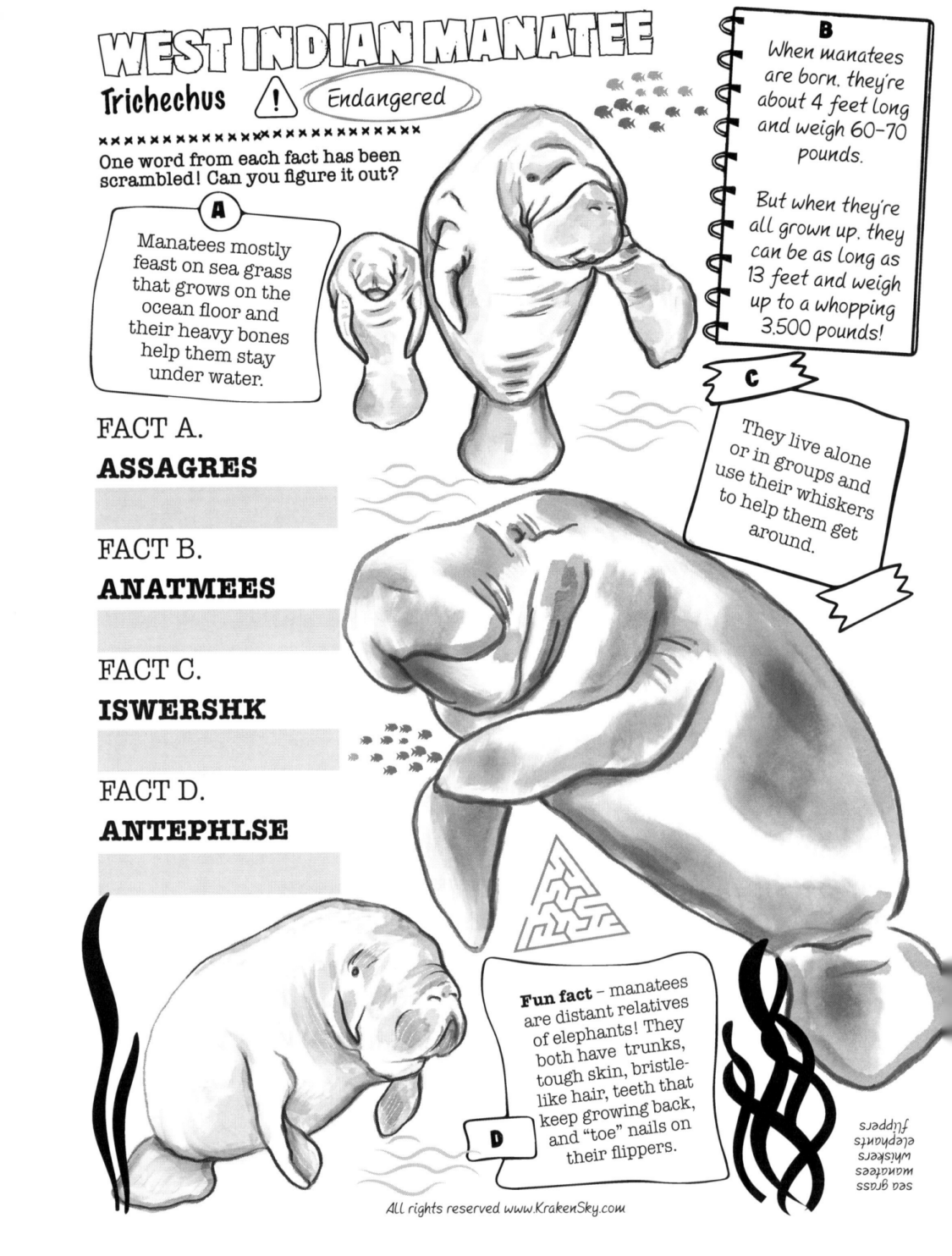

THRESHER SHARK

The thresher shark stuns its prey by using its elongated tail as a whipping weapon.

Angel sharks love munching on fish parties like bluefish, baby tuna, and mackerel. Besides fish, they sometimes enjoy a squid or cuttlefish snack, and if they're feeling adventurous, they might even nibble on a crustacean or maybe a seabird. It's like they've got a whole buffet under the sea!

Did You Know?

The bat ray has a sneaky spine in its tail, but don't worry, it's not a troublemaker. The ray only brings out the spine if it feels scared or someone tries to bother it. If you're swimming in shallow sand and want to give the bat ray some space, just shuffle your feet – it's like doing a little dance that lets them know you're coming without any surprises!

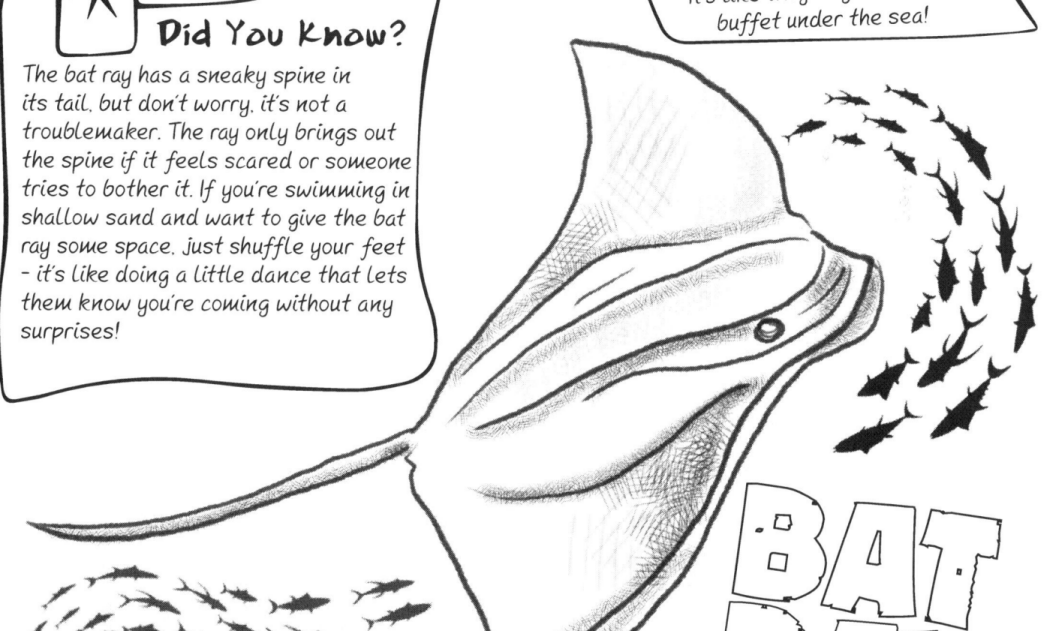

BAT RAY

WHICH OF THESE 5 FACTS IS NOT TRUE?

1. Shark skin feels similar to sandpaper

2. Great white sharks can go weeks without eating

3. Sharks can see in the dark better than cats

4. Each whale shark's spot pattern is different

5. Sharks have bones that float

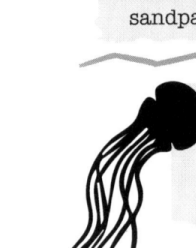

Word Bank for the puzzles below: Mako • White • Sand Tiger • Hammerhead • Nurse • Whale • Lemon • Bull • Ocean • Shark Teeth

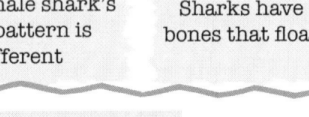

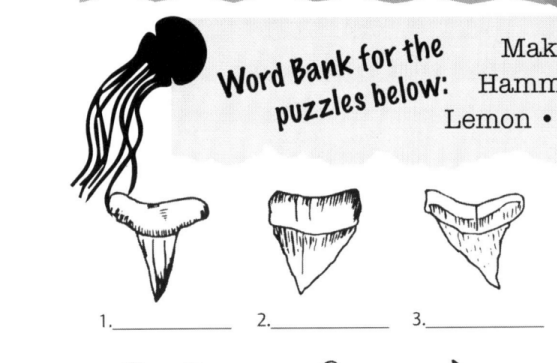

Can you guess what shark these come from? Use the word bank above!

False fact is 5: Sharks do not have bones!

1. Lemon Shark 2. White Shark 3. Bull Shark 4. Mako Shark 5. Nurse Shark 6. Sand Tiger Shark 7. Whale Shark 8. Hammerhead

All rights & permissions: Www.KrakenSky.com

ENDANGERED

FLORIDA PANTHER

Puma concolor coryi

KEY DEER

Odocoileus virginianus clavium

ENDANGERED

Lives only in the Florida Keys and is the smallest North American deer species.

? Florida panthers are the larger of Florida's two native cat species.

The other native cat is the bobcat.

Use your imagination to finish creating a creature all your own!

Back in the 1970s, there were only around 20 to 30 Florida panthers living in the wild. But now, there are a bit over 200 of them roaming around in their natural habitat.*

*www.nwf.org

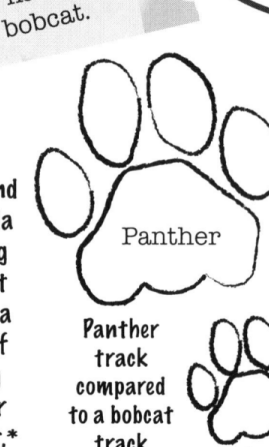

Panther track compared to a bobcat track

Panther

Bobcat

All rights reserved www.KrakenSky.com

MONARCH BUTTERFLY

Danaus plexippus

The beautiful bright orange and black colors on monarch butterflies is a warning to predators that they are toxic!

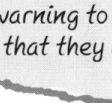

Toxic means it's harmful and can make you sick or hurt you in some way.

#DYK Monarch caterpillars ONLY feed on milkweed plants, and they prefer certain types, like common milkweed and swamp milkweed.

Like other butterflies, monarchs are important pollinators, especially during their flights looking for food.

When a pollinator, like a bee or a butterfly, visits a flower, tiny grains called pollen stick to their bodies. Then, when the pollinator flies to another flower, some of that pollen rubs off onto the new flower, helping the flower make seeds and grow more flowers!

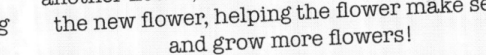

MONARCH BUTTERFLIES

Monarch butterflies are often seen as symbols of beauty and transformation.

Do You Remember?

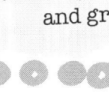

The beautiful colors mean the insect is _____

Pollinators rub _____ on new flowers.

Besides a butterfly, give an example of another pollinator _____.

The only food monarch caterpillars eat is _____.

Color me!
Wings are bright orange with black lines and edges!

Monarch populations have been getting smaller because of habitat loss, lawn chemical use, climate change, and other factors.

You can help! Plant milkweed to create butterfly-friendly areas!

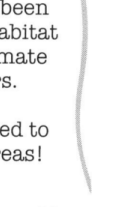

Toxic, pollen, bee, milkweed

All rights & permissions: www.KrakenSky.com

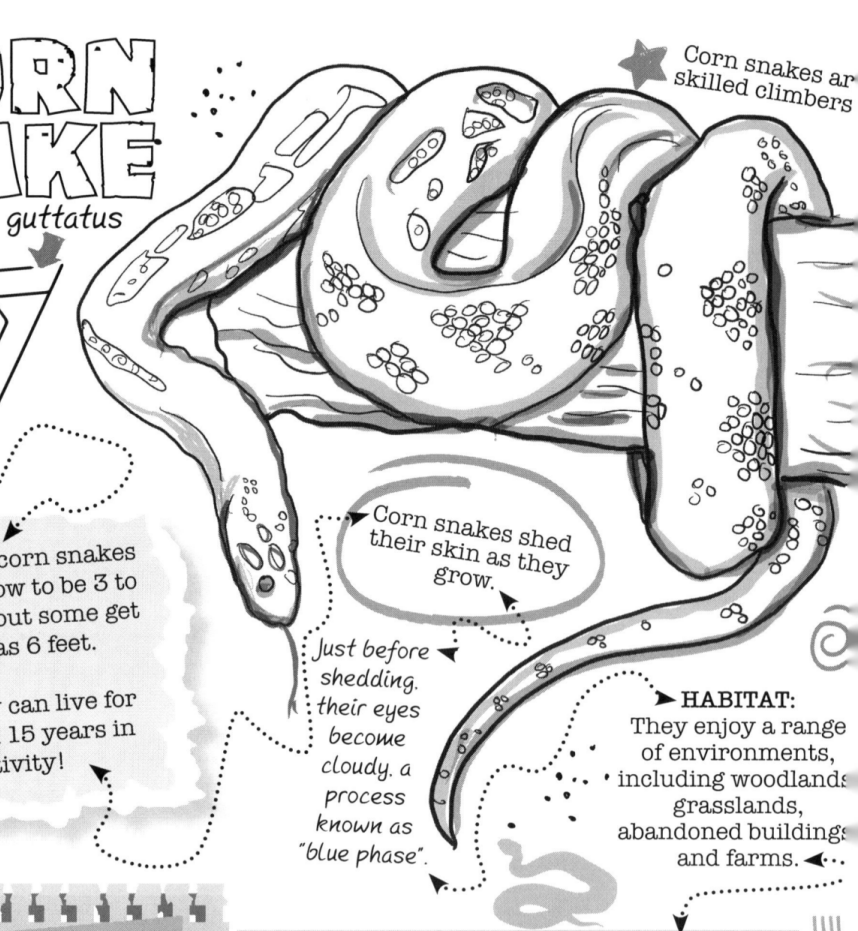

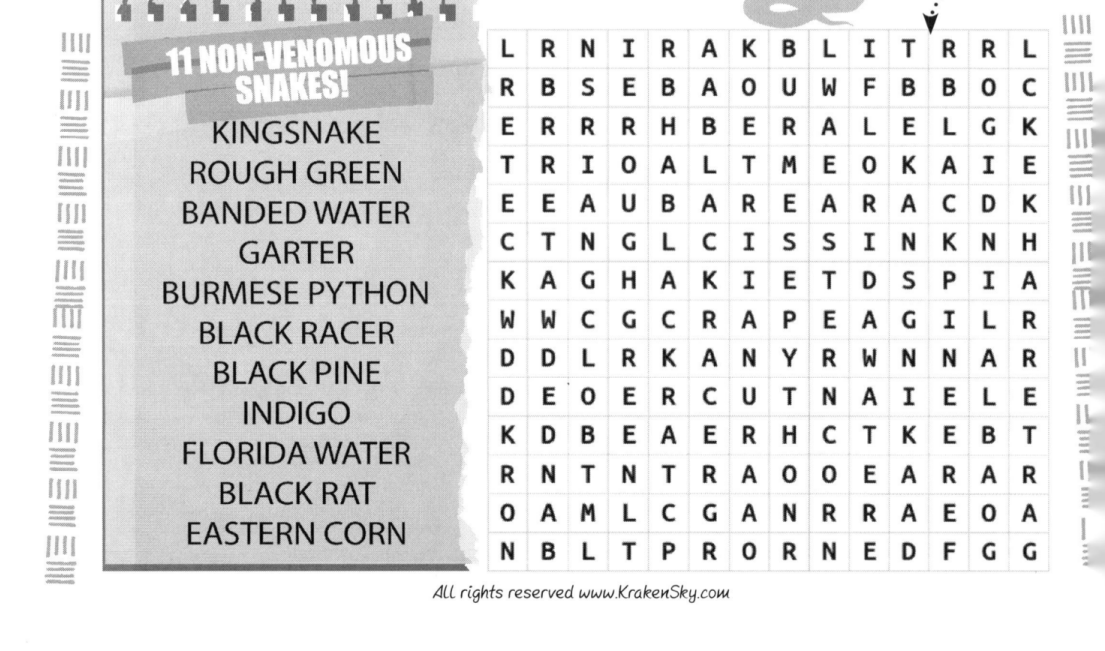

All rights reserved www.KrakenSky.com

POLYPHEMUS MOTH

BARKING TREE FROG

FLORIDA BLACK BEAR

Ursus americanus floridanus

Can you fill in the two missing directions?

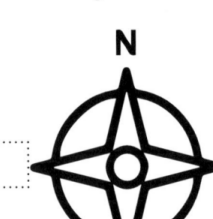

Our special guest! Black bears are the only bears that live in Florida!

Weight:
Adult male - 250 - 350 pounds
Adult female - 130 - 180 pounds

Diet:
Mostly plants, some insects and a very small amount of meat (small animals like opossum or armadillos)

Word Scramble

RTNOH

HSTOU

ETAS

SWET

RED WOLF

Canis rufus

Federally-designated Endangered

Weight:
80 pounds

Diet:
Small animals and deer

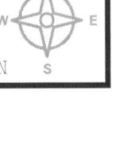

NORTH, SOUTH, EAST, WEST

All rights reserved www.KrakenSky.com

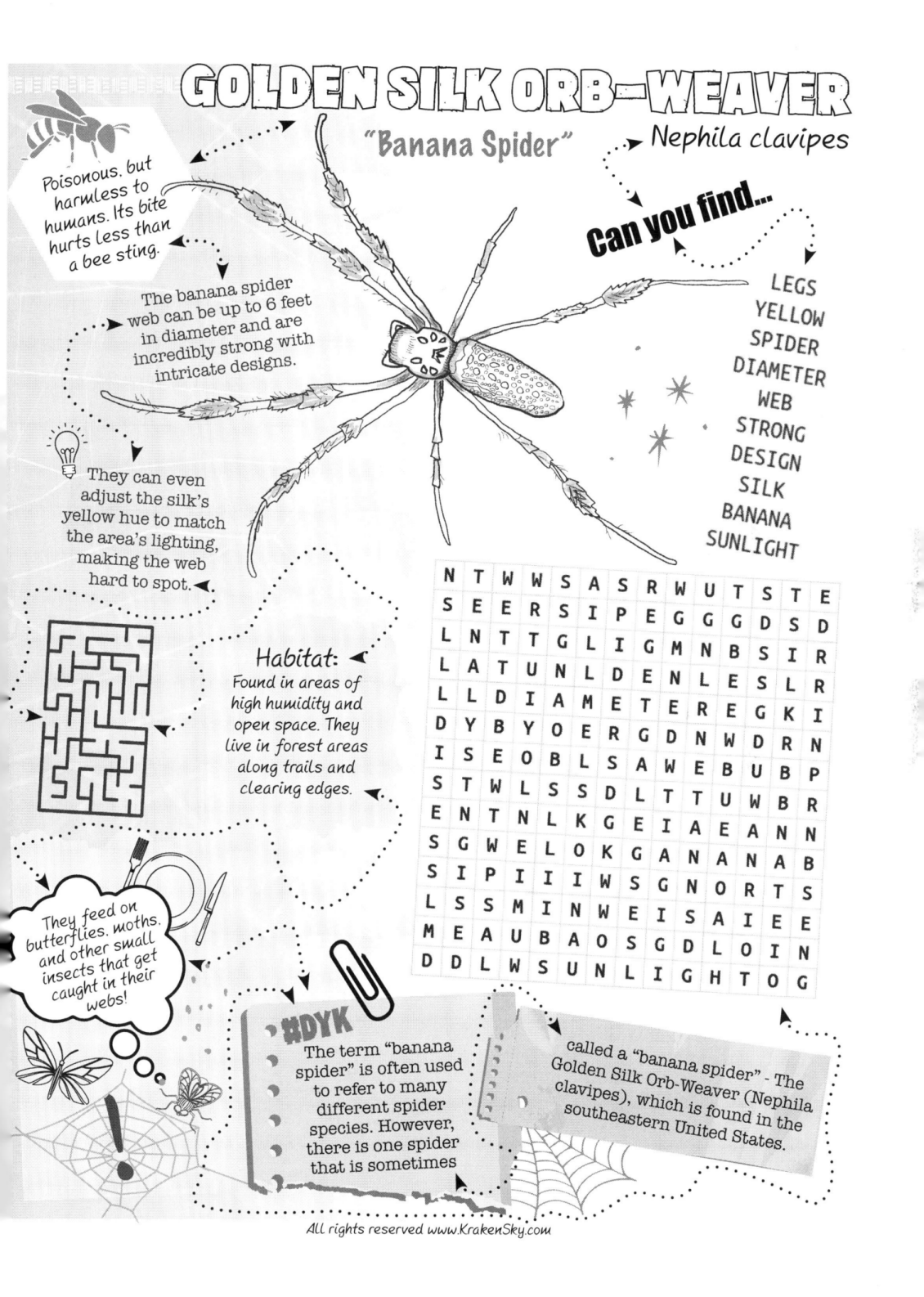

MARSH RABBIT

Sylvilagus palustris

A marsh rabbit is a small cottontail rabbit that is a strong swimmer and found only by areas of water.

Weight: 2.2-2.6 pounds / Length 17 inches.

Weird but true!

Although they can hop like all rabbits, one very unusual habit of marsh rabbits is that they walk on all fours, placing each foot down alternately like a cat!

OPOSSUM

Didelphis virginiana

Florida has just one kind of animal with a pouch to carry its babies, and it's called the Virginia opossum.

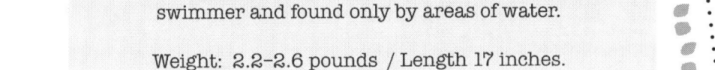

BARKING TREE FROG

Hyla gratiosa

Color Me! I'm bright green with a yellow stripe on my sides.

Sometimes called the "rain frog" because its barking call is usually heard during rainstorms.

WILD HOGS

Sus scrofa

#DYK that wild boars are super smart? They can remember where they've found food before, which helps them survive in the wild.

All rights reserved www.KrakenSky.com

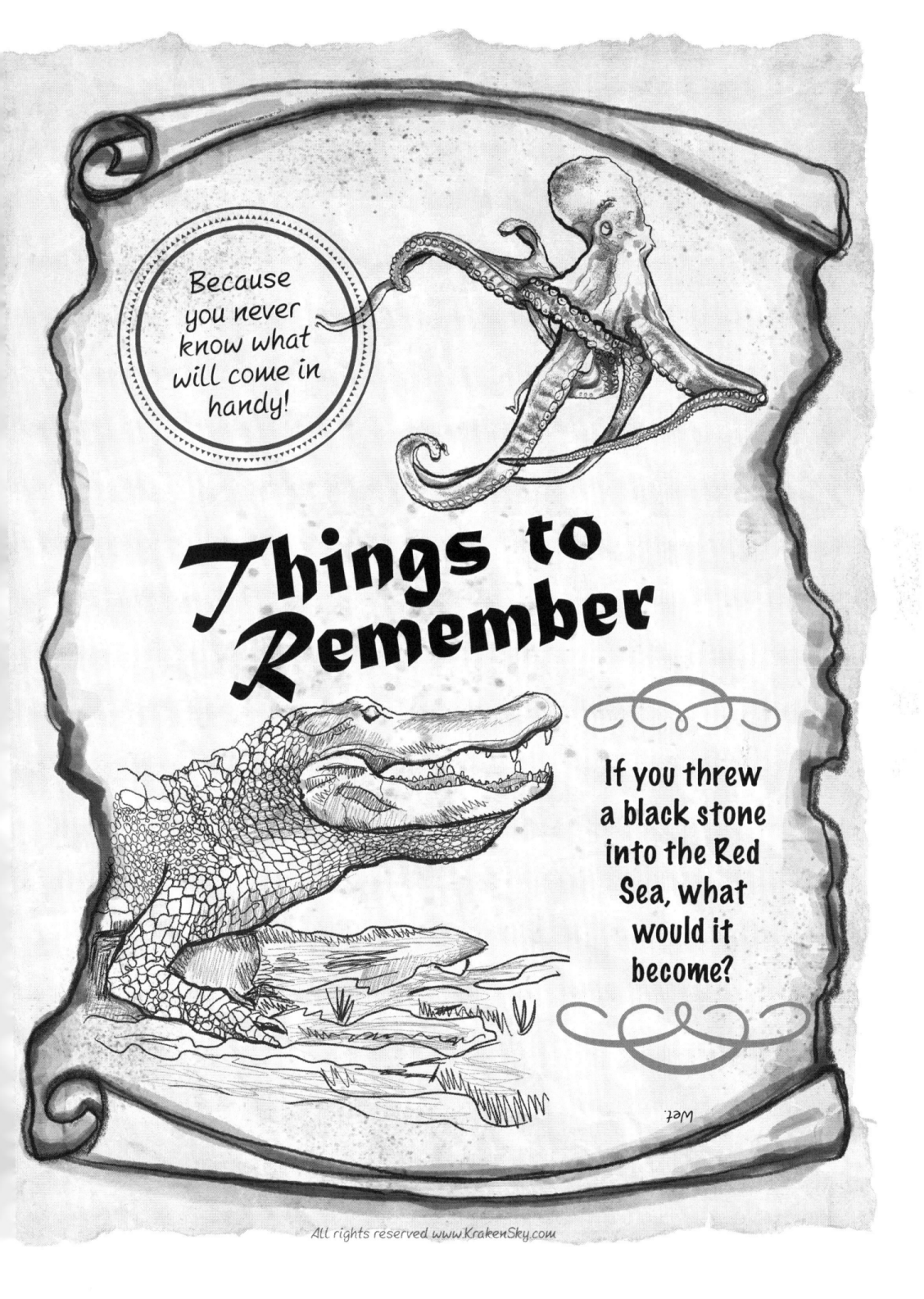

SHELLING: Pro Tips *When is the best TIME to find seashells?*

A	B	C	D	E	F	G	H	I	J	K	L	M	N	O	P	Q	R	S	T	U	V	W	X	Y	Z
≙	≐	Ⅱ	λ	∟	⌐	┌	┐	∩	Ʊ	···	···	⋮	∴	∵	‖	∷	∠	◁	□	∪	△	□	□	□	↗

SECRET MESSAGE:

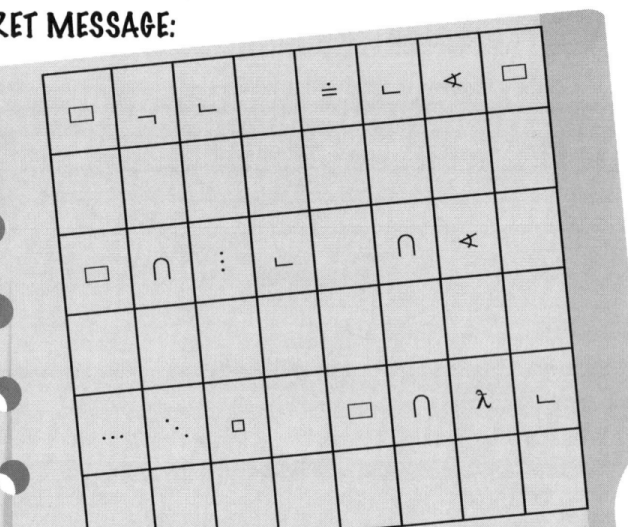

ARROWHEAD SAND DOLLAR

SEA BISCUIT SAND DOLLAR

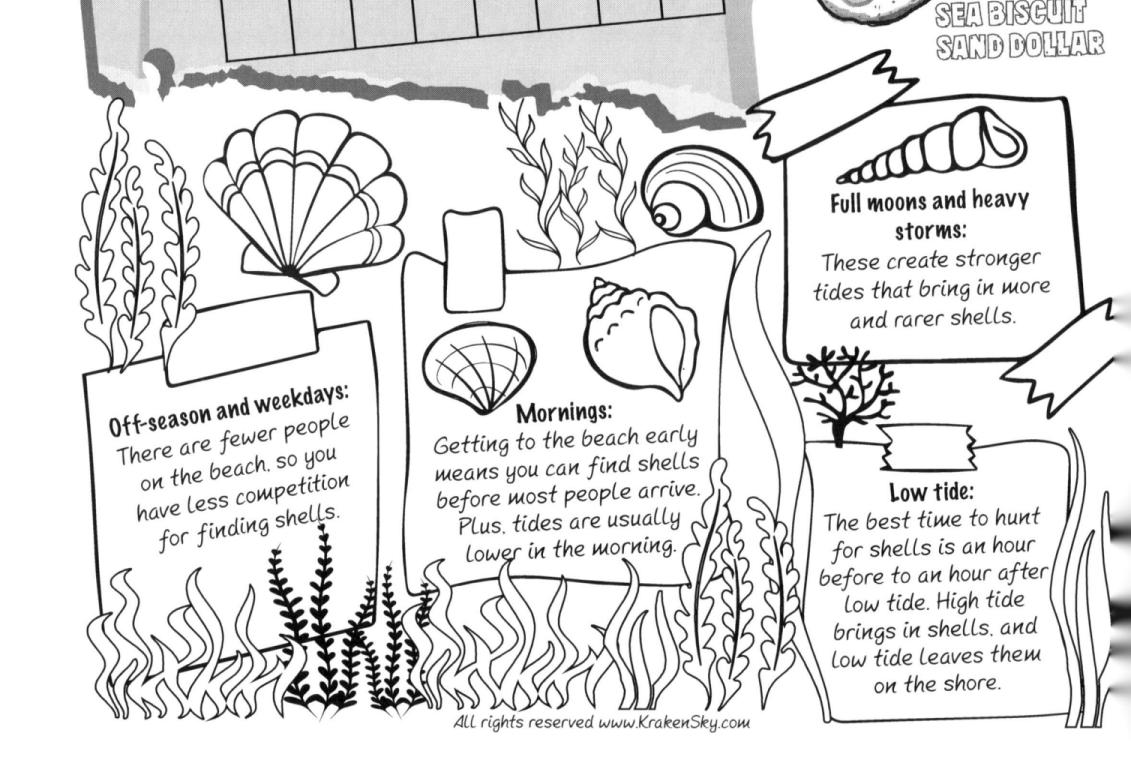

Full moons and heavy storms:
These create stronger tides that bring in more and rarer shells.

Off-season and weekdays:
There are fewer people on the beach, so you have less competition for finding shells.

Mornings:
Getting to the beach early means you can find shells before most people arrive. Plus, tides are usually lower in the morning.

Low tide:
The best time to hunt for shells is an hour before to an hour after low tide. High tide brings in shells, and low tide leaves them on the shore.

All rights reserved www.KrakenSky.com

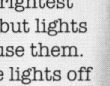

ALLIGATOR =OR= CROCODILE?

Some differences between

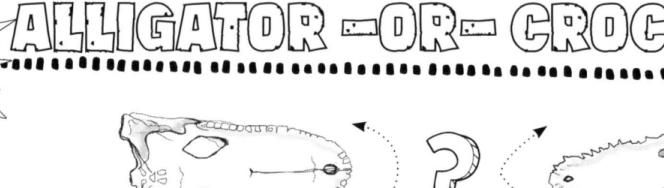

Alligator		**Crocodile**
Black or gray on top, cream-colored belly		Mostly green or brown
U-shaped		V-shape
Smaller, 8 to 15 feet in length		Larger, 10 to 16+ feet
Freshwater like swamps, marshes, and lakes		Saltwater like rivers, estuaries, and coastal areas
Southeastern United States, and eastern China.		Africa, Asia, the Americas, and Australia
More shy and stay away from humans if possible		More aggressive and may be more likely to attack humans

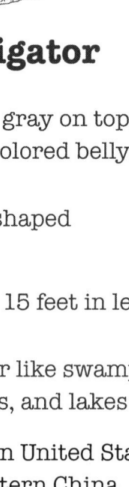

DO NOT FEED

Crocodiles and alligators can go short distances FAST, especially in water.

On land, they can run 5 to 9 miles per hour depending on size, age, and type of ground!

To compare, an human's jogging speed is usually 4-6 miles an hour, running is 6+ miles an hour.

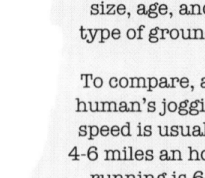

NO SWIMMING

Aggressive: ready or likely to attack!

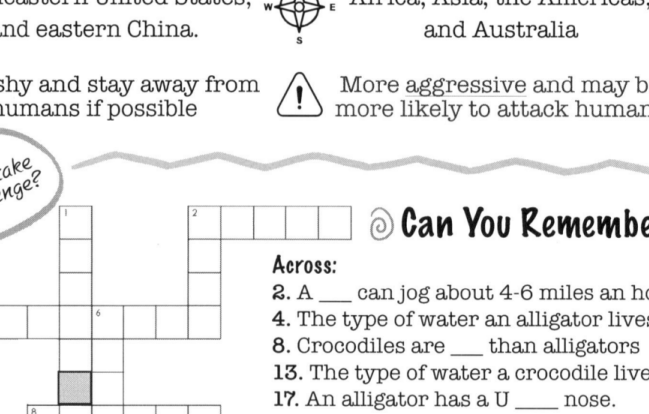

Can You Remember?

Across:
2. A ___ can jog about 4-6 miles an hour
4. The type of water an alligator lives in
8. Crocodiles are ___ than alligators
13. The type of water a crocodile lives in
17. An alligator has a U ___ nose.

Down:
1. A crocodile is mostly green or ___.
2. An alligator can run 5-9 miles per ___
3. One place you can find crocodiles
6. Vocab word that means ready to attack
12. Are a type of fresh water area

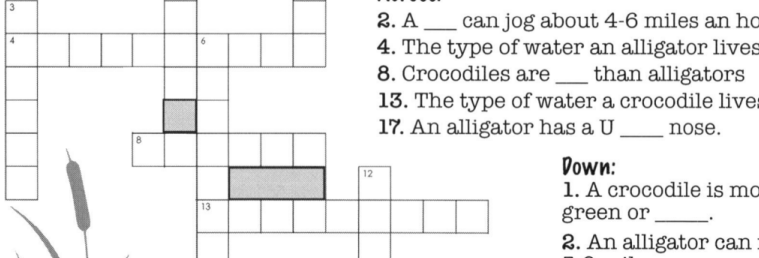

All rights reserved www.KrakenSky.com

A: human, fresh water, larger, salt water, shaped. D: brown, hour, Africa, aggressive, marshes

An invasive species is a plant or animal brought from somewhere else that is bad for new place it lives in.

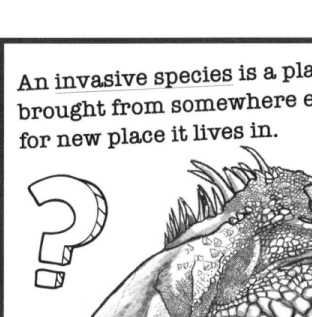

How do they get moved?
Sometimes they are accidentally hiding in shipping containers, they were released or escaped pets, in the ballast water on ships, even in construction wood.

Example: BURMESE PYTHONS

Burmese pythons eat many other animals that are an important part of the natural ecosystem.

They also take food away from other animals that need it to survive.

In 5-7 years, a Burmese python can eat:

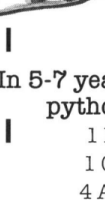

- 1 Raccoon
- 1 Opossum
- 4 Alligators
- 5 American Coots (bird)
- 6 Blue Herons (bird)
- 8 Ibises (bird)
- 10 Squirrels
- 15 Rabbits
- 15 Wrens (bird)
- 30 Cotton Rats
- 72 Mice

What does INVASIVE SPECIES mean?

Just in the sate of Florida, there are over 500 invasive plant and animal species.

Because the environment is so warm. Plants and animals can easily adapt to their new home, including:

**BURMESE PYTHONS
FERAL HOGS – CANE TOADS
LIONFISH – CUBAN TREE FROGS
GIANT AFRICAN LAND SNAILS
IGUANAS – GREEN MUSSELS
TEGU LIZARDS – BRAZILIAN PEPPER-TREE
SKUNKVINE – RUNNING BAMBOOS**

Can You Match The Scrambled Word?

LIONFISH	**PONSYTH**
IGUANAS	**NASUAIG**
SKUNKVINE	**ANADSECTO**
CANE TOADS	**OFISNLIH**
PYTHONS	**KUSVINENK**
LIZARDS	**ZADSRLI**

Be a Citizen Scientist!

Report an invasive species to: National Invasive Species Information Center
www.invasivespeciesinfo.gov

Download the free smartphone app: Wild Spotter - Mapping Invasives in America's Wild Places

You Can Help!

Seek by iNaturalist is a kid-friendly app that allows young scientists to earn badges while they identify plants and animals from photos!

All rights & permissions: Www.KrakenSky.com

SHELLING: Pro Tips

Where are the best places to LOOK for seashells?

Talk to locals:
They can give you tips on the best shelling spots.

Avoid busy areas:
These beaches are often plowed in the morning, making it hard to find shells. If you are at one of these beaches, go early before they plow.

Check seaweed and sea grass:
Shells can be mixed in with these.

High tide line:
Look along the line left by high tide. This is where you'll find the most shells, along with some trash and other debris.

SECRET MESSAGE:

Code:

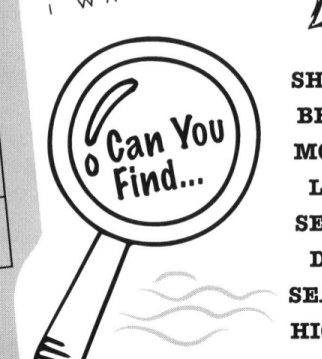

SHELLING
BEACHES
MORNING
LOCALS
SEAWEED
DEBRIS
SEA GRASS
HIGH TIDE

A	B	C	D	E	F	G	H	I	J	K	L	M	N	O	P	Q	R	S	T	U	V	W	X	Y	Z
≙	≐	Ⅱ	λ	∟	⌐	⌐	∩	U	…	…	∶	∴	∵	‖	∵	∠	◁	□	U	△	◻	□	◻	↗

All rights reserved www.KrakenSky.com

1. Alligators Can't Climb.
True or False?

2. Alligators can't see very well, except underwater.
True or False?

3. Alligators can't catch people or prey when they run zig-zag.
True or False?

4. Both alligators and crocodiles have a purple-ish liquid that naturally foams around their eyes to works like sunscreen for their eyeballs.
True or False?

THE AMERICAN ALLIGATOR
Alligator mississippiensis
Lifespan: 30 – 50 years

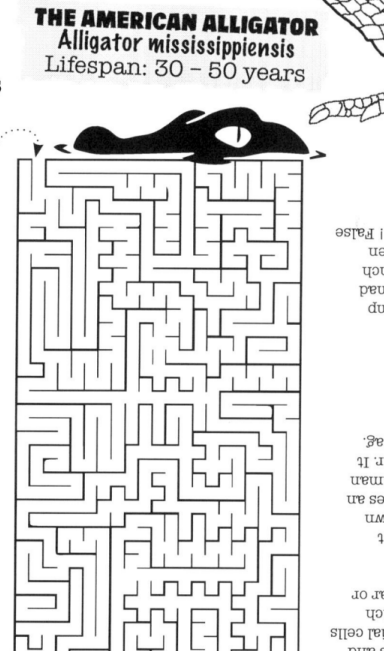

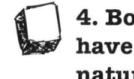

5. Alligators can't jump.
True or False?

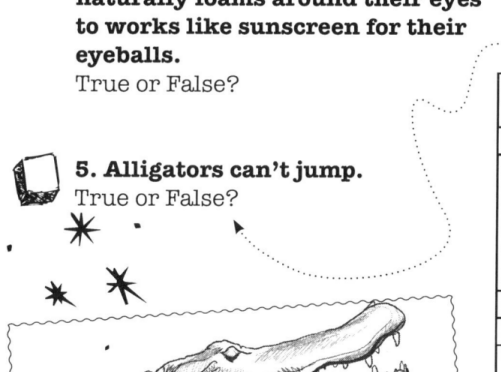

1. Alligators have been observed climbing over walls to escape being caught or to reach water. False.

2. Alligators eyes are located on either side of their head, giving them a wide view of any area. They can see far distances and their eyes even have special cells to allow in more light, which means better vision in near or full darkness! False.

3. Alligators are really fast animals and can chase down what they want at 5-9 miles an hour! In comparison, a human runs about 6 miles an hour. It doesn't matter if you zig-zag. False.

4. I totally made this up. Absolutely false.

5. Alligators can really jump well, and those legs have mad jump power. They can launch themselves up to 6 feet even from lying completely still! False.

All rights & permissions: Www.KrakenSky.com

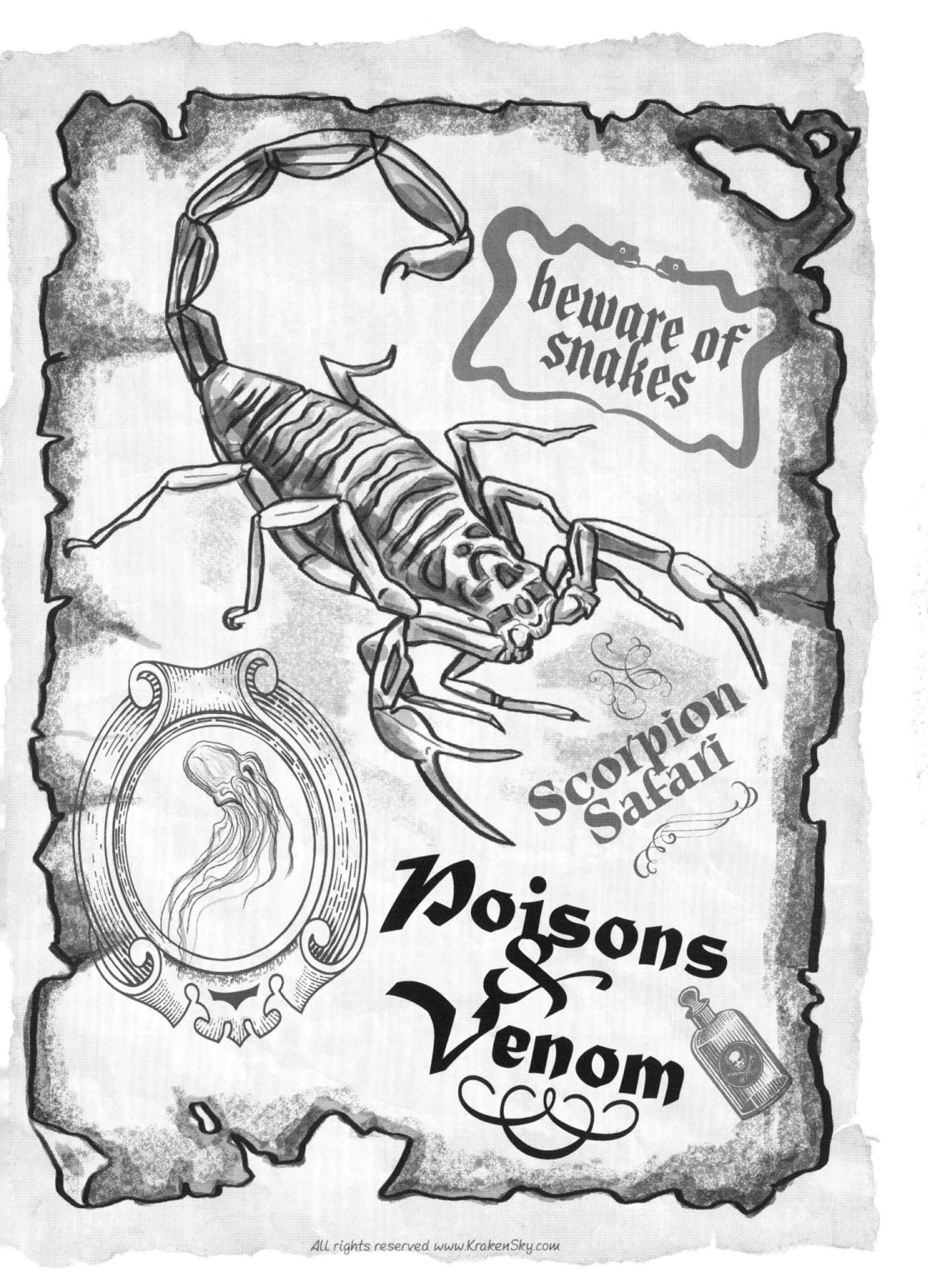

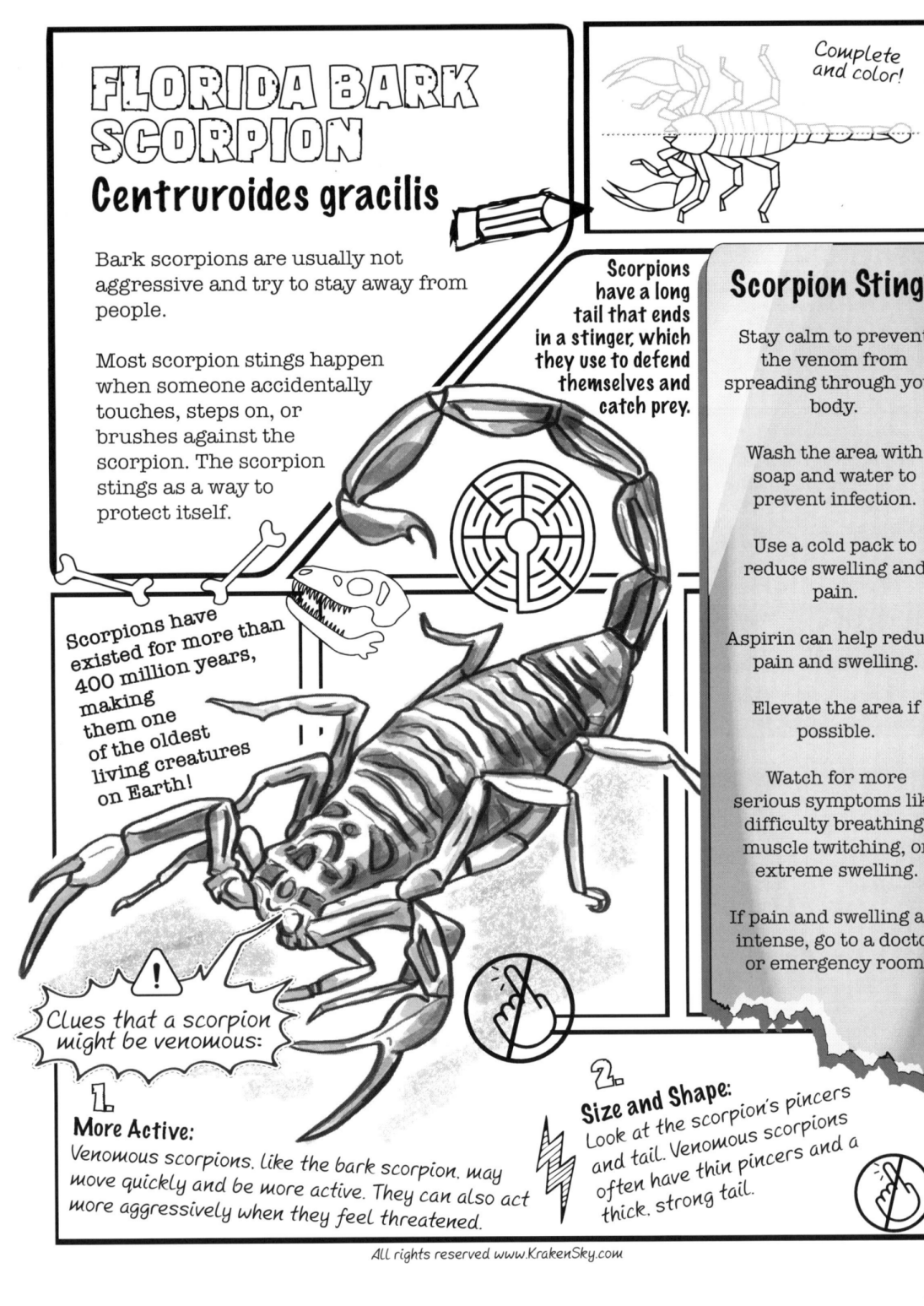

SCORPION SAFARI Game

Draw the images to finish the pattern!

Did you know... Scorpions can glow bright under ultraviolet (UV) light!

Go On A Real Scorpion Safari!

Try going for a walk in the woods with a black light flashlight at night (with an adult) for a real scorpion safari!

All rights reserved www.KrakenSky.com

FLORIDA SNAKE TRIVIA: Is It Venomous?

YES / NO

1. _____ Cottonmouth (A.K.A. Water Moccasin)
2. _____ Eastern Corn Snake
3. _____ Dusky Pygmy Rattlesnake
4. _____ Black Pine Snake
5. _____ Eastern Coral Snake
6. _____ Black Rat Snake
7. _____ Florida Water Snake
8. _____ Eastern Diamondback Rattlesnake
9. _____ Eastern Coachwhip
10. _____ Black Racer
11. _____ Southern Copperhead
12. _____ Timber Rattlesnake

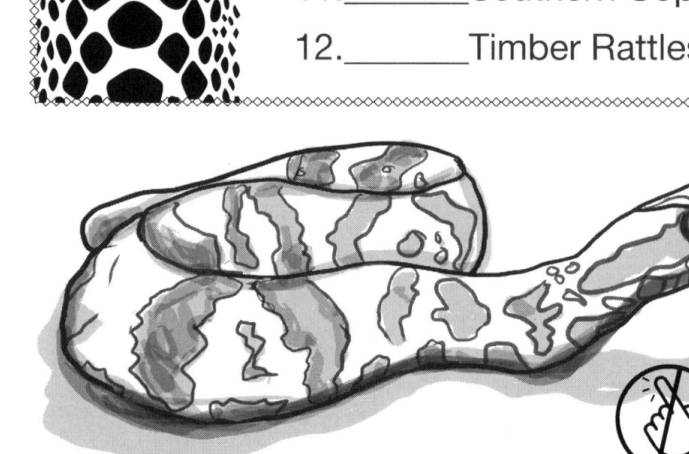

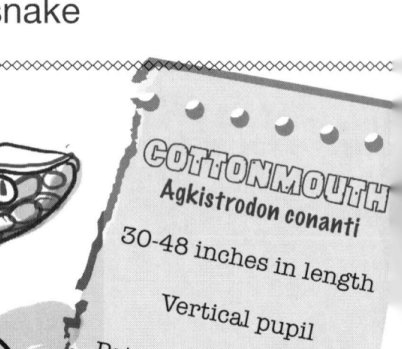

VENOMOUS! Cottonmouth bites can be very dangerous!

1. Yes, 2. No, 3. Yes, 4. No, 5. Yes, 6. No, 7. No, 8. Yes, 9. No, 10. No, 11. Yes, 12. Yes

All rights & permissions: Www.KrakenSky.com

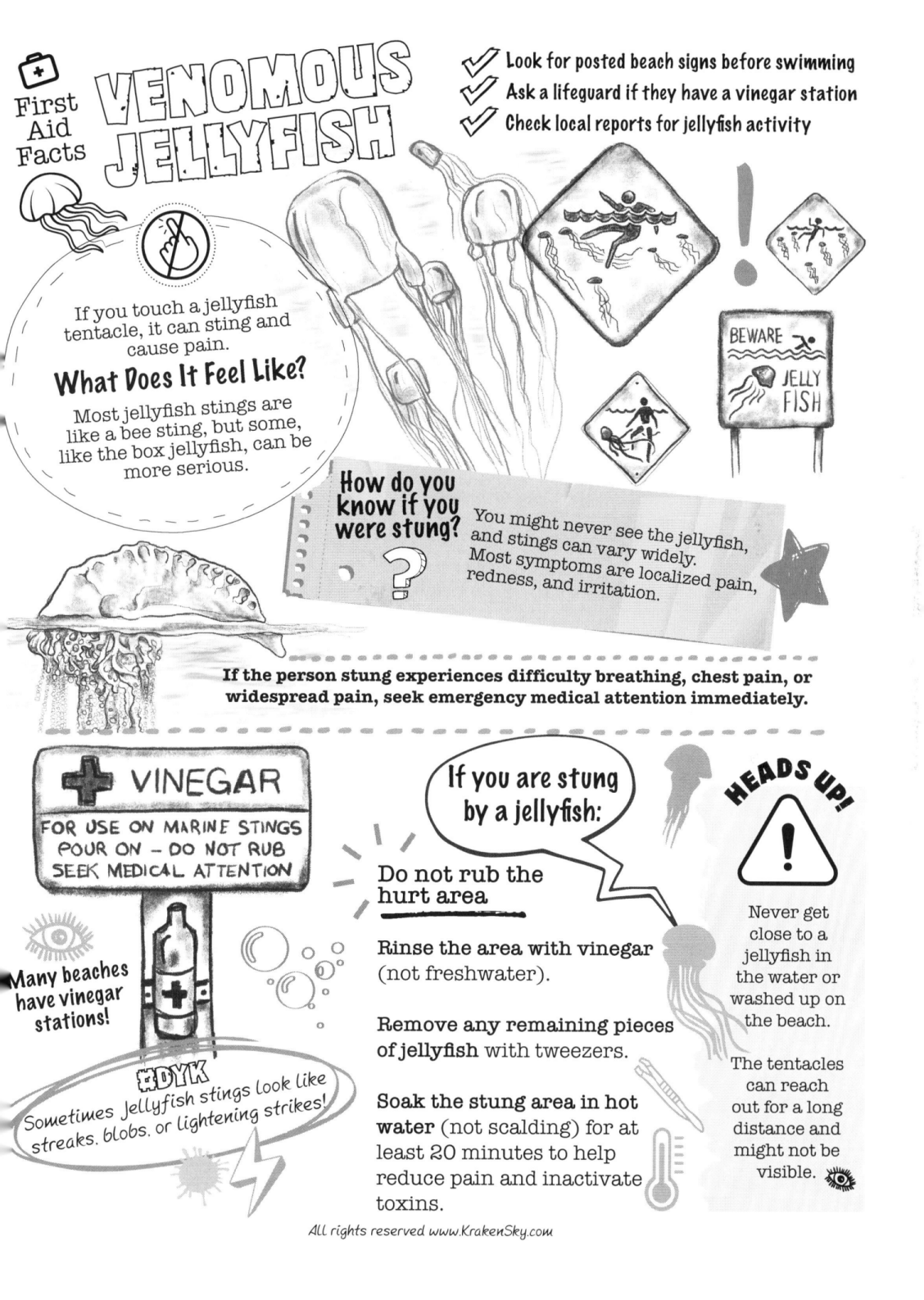

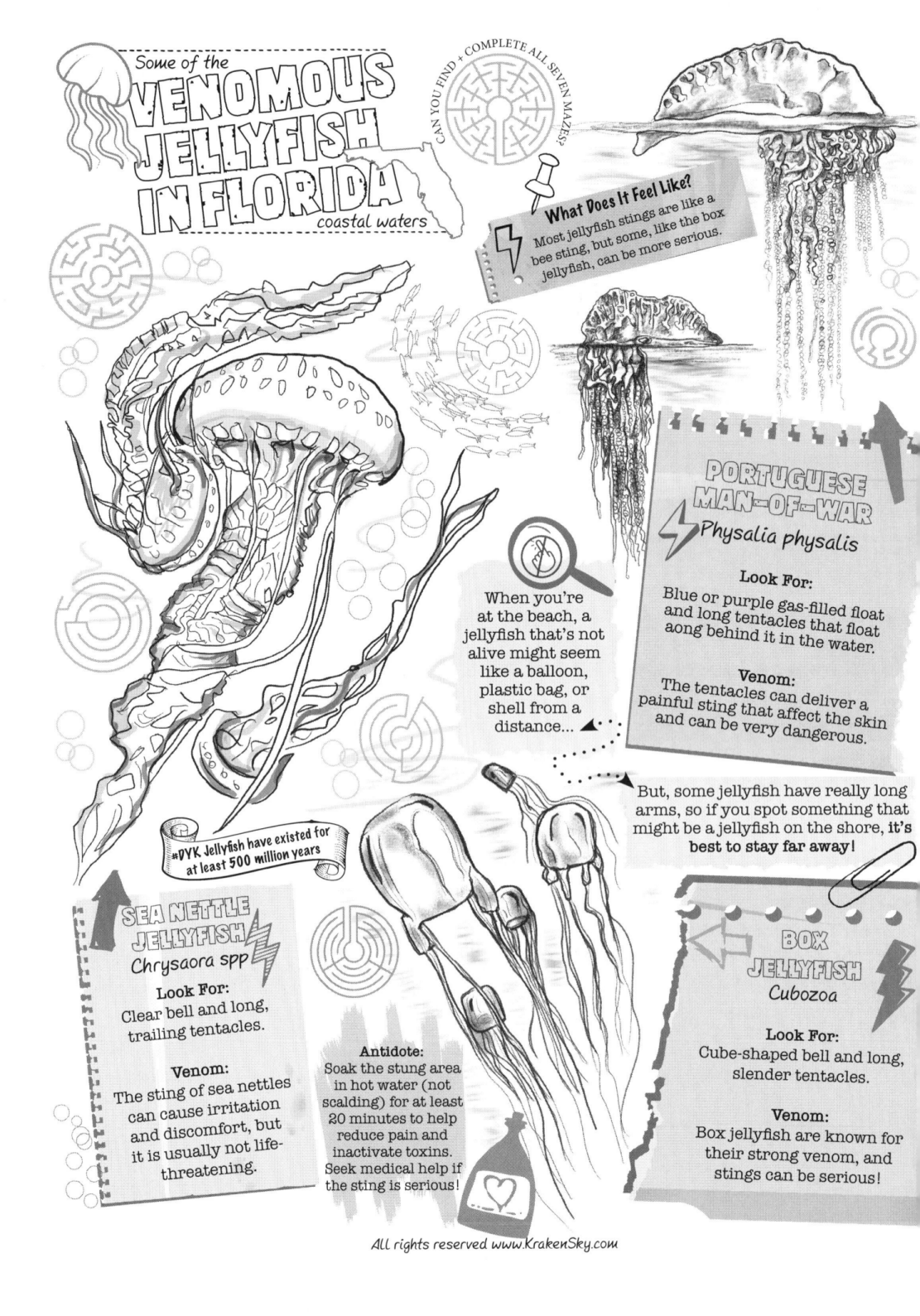

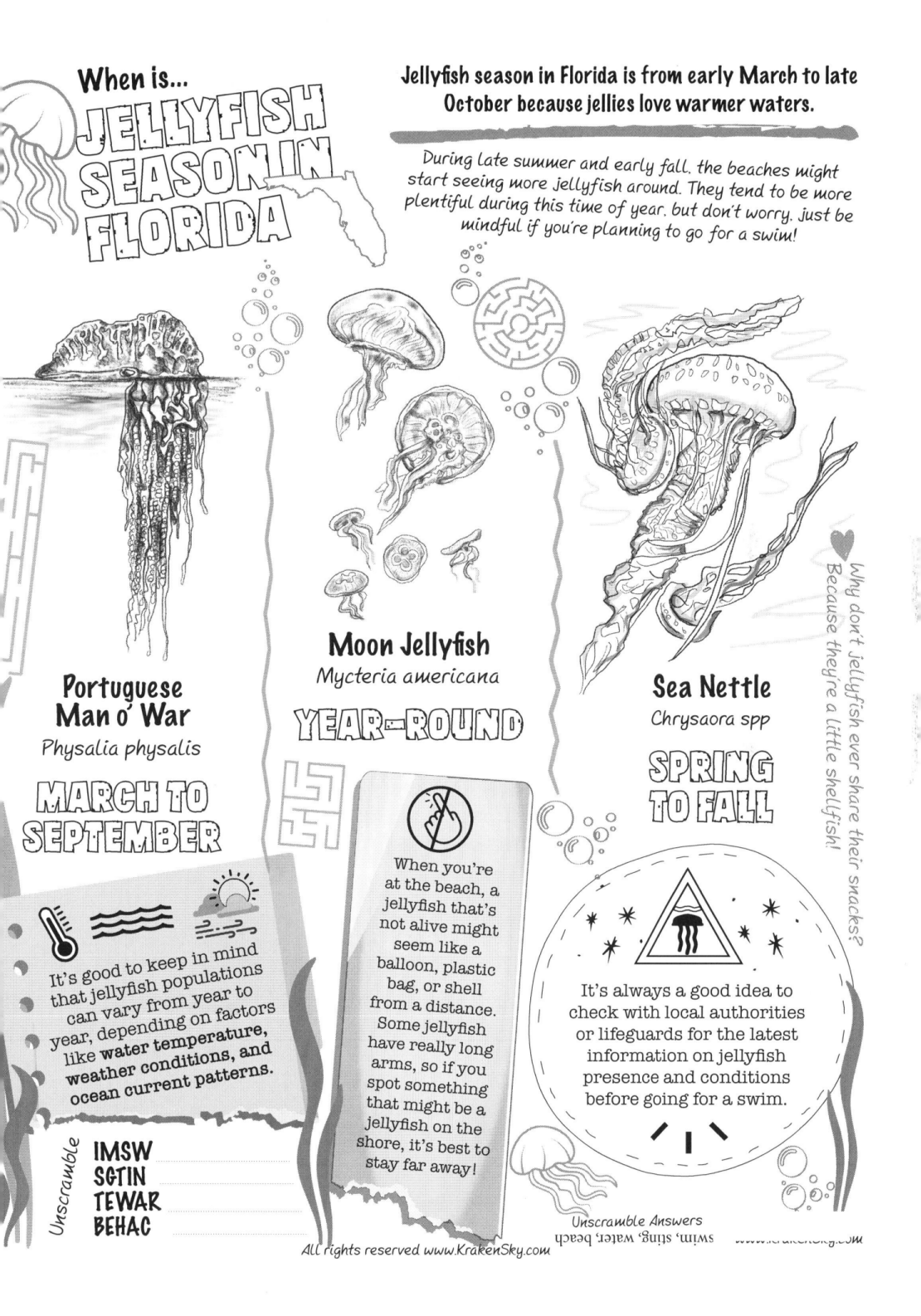

POISON IVY

POISON OAK

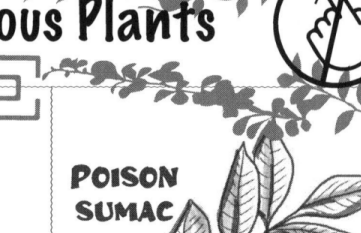

POISON SUMAC

Poison Ivy	Poison Oak	Poison Sumac
Leaves of Three, Let Them Be	**Leaves of Three, Let Them Be**	**Best Clue: Red stems**
Oval-shaped, glossy leaves	Vary in shape	Oval leaves that come to a point
No thorns	Sometimes hairy or fuzzy	Wavy or smooth
Can be reddish in spring and fall	Shiny and green	Parallel rows
Saw-toothed edges	Can have a red tint	May change color like fall leaves
Grows low as a bush or high as a climbing vine	Dry, sandy areas	Small tree
	Vine or bush	Likes wet areas like swamps, ponds, and mud
	Found along paths and trails in the woods, but can live anywhere	
Very common	Less common than poison ivy	Poison sumac isn't as common as poison ivy or poison oak

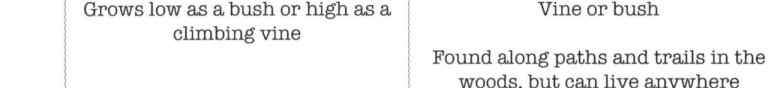

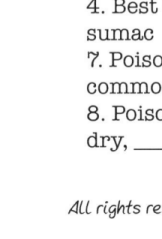

Across:
1. Leaves of _____, let them be
3. Oil in plants that makes you itchy
6. Wear long _____ in the woods

Down:
2. Poison sumac grows in parallel _____
4. Best clue for poison sumac
7. Poison ivy is _____ common
8. Poison oak likes dry, _____ areas

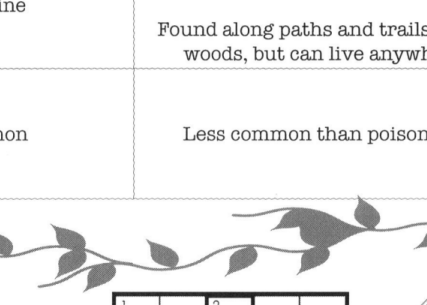

Wear long sleeves and pants in wooded areas, and stay on the cleared path to avoid touching plants unless you are sure they aren't poisonous!

The oil in plants like poison ivy, poison oak, and poison sumac is called **urushiol (yoo-ROO-she-ol)**. If you accidentally touch these plants, it's super important to wash your skin really well so you don't get a red, itchy rash that can stick around for weeks!

All rights reserved www.KrakenSky.com

Three, urushiol, sleeves, rows, red stems, sandy

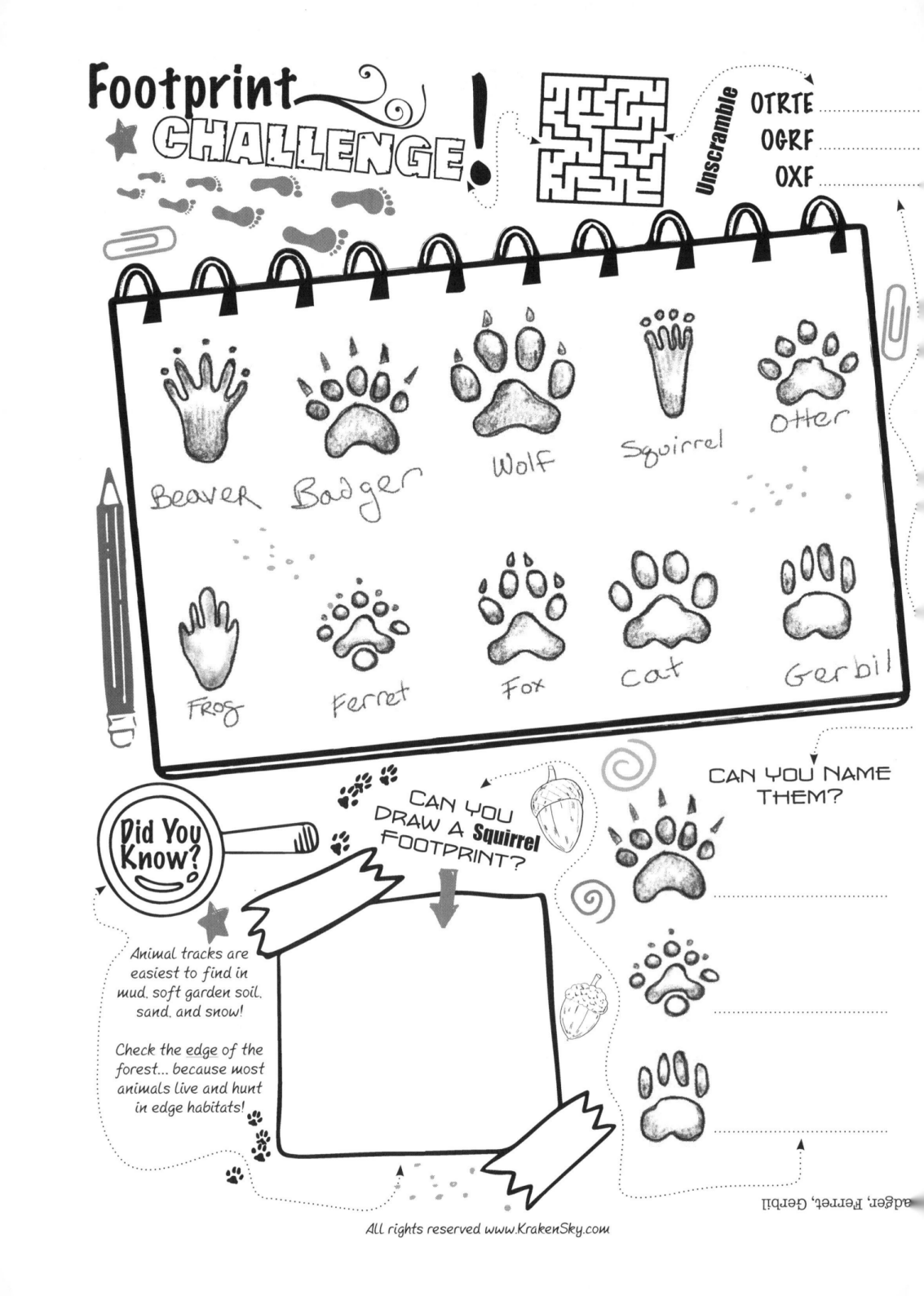

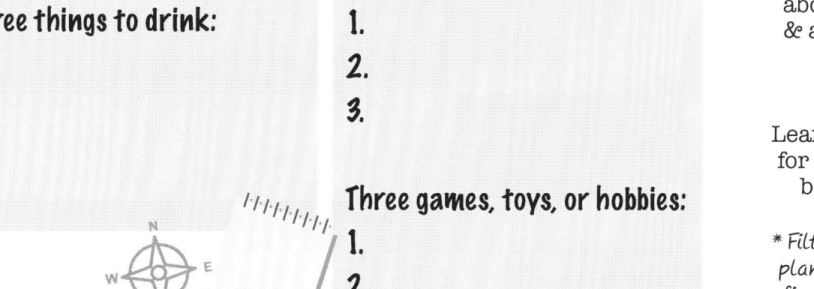

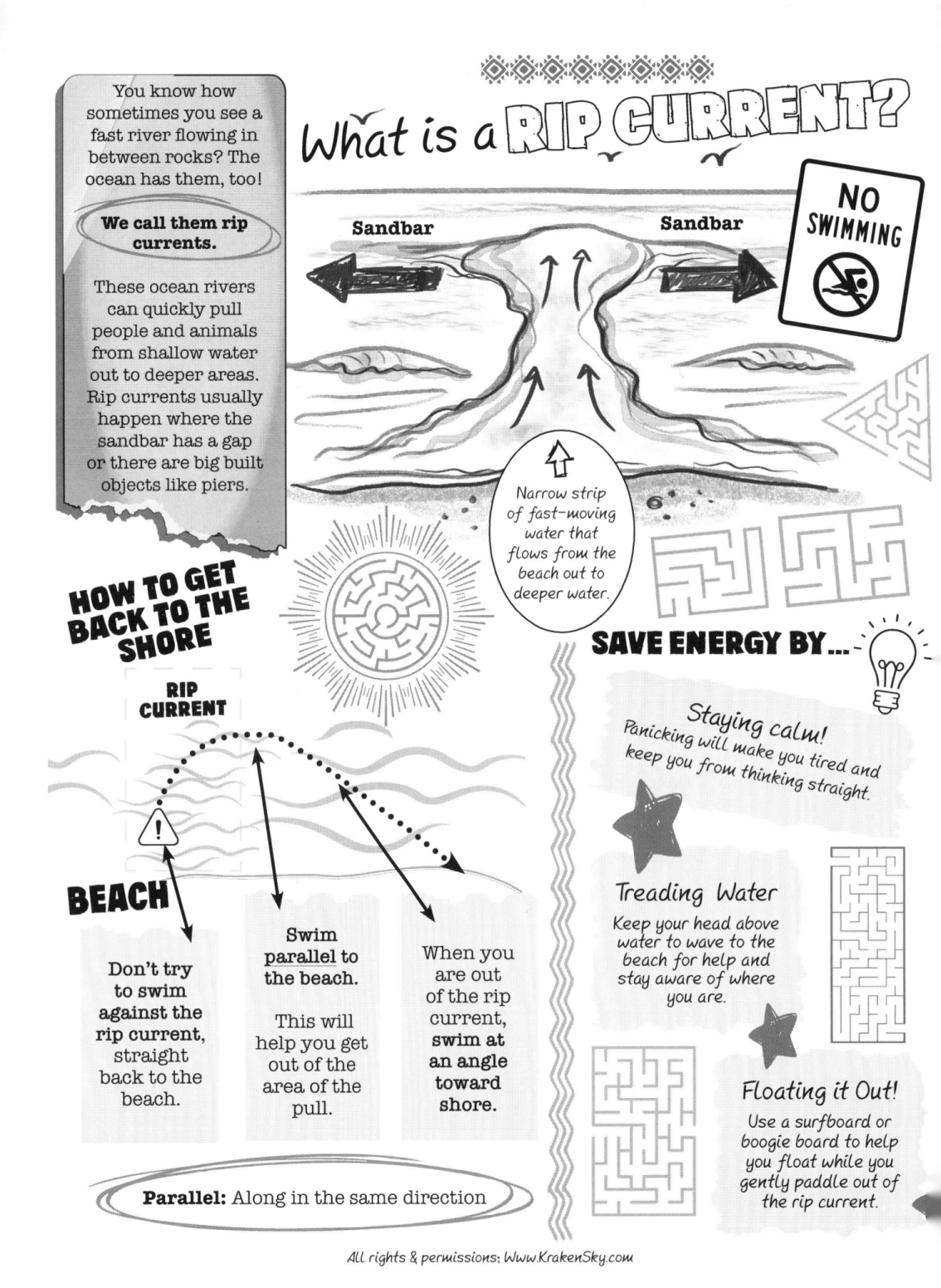

Tips:

Create each knot on a flat surface. It's easier to see the pattern that way.

♥ Take your time! ♥

Don't pull any part of the knot tight until the full pattern is created.

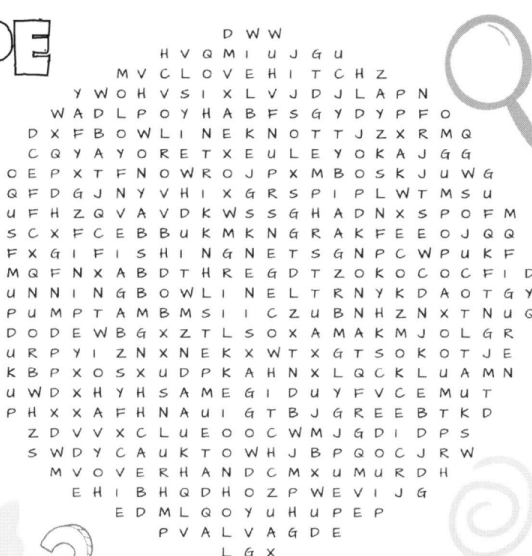

Overhand Knot

Figure Eight Knot

Cow Hitch

Clove Hitch

Pieces of old ropes and knots that are 15,000 to 17,000 years old show that people have been using knots for a very long time—long before they invented the wheel or the axe!

Knots have been super important for making things like fishing nets, hunting traps, and baskets.

Even though they might seem simple, knots are the key part of these inventions.

Can You Find...

OVERHAND – FIGURE EIGHT – COW HITCH CLOVE HITCH – SHEEPSHANK KNOT BOWLINE KNOT – RUNNING BOWLINE – ROPES FISHING NETS – HUNTING TRAPS – BASKETS

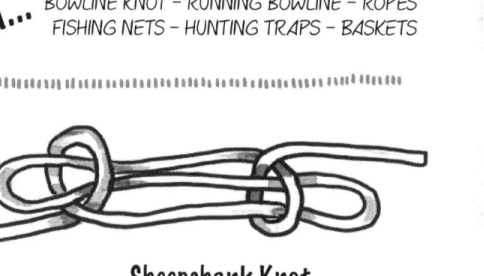

Sheepshank Knot

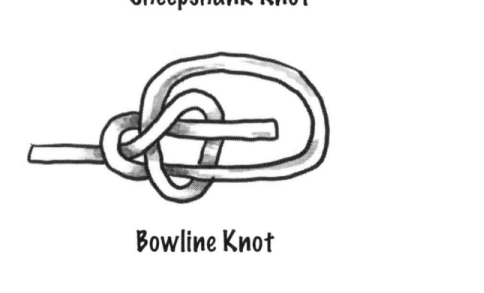

Bowline Knot

Running Bowline

All rights & permissions: Www.KrakenSky.com

MORSE CODE

.. .-.. --- ...- . ...- -. - .. -. --. ... .-.. .-.. ...

... .- -. -.. -.- --- .-.. .-.. .- .-. ... .- .-. . -... . .- ..- - .. ..-. ..- .-..

-- --- .-. ... . -.-. --- -.. . .. .-. ..- -.

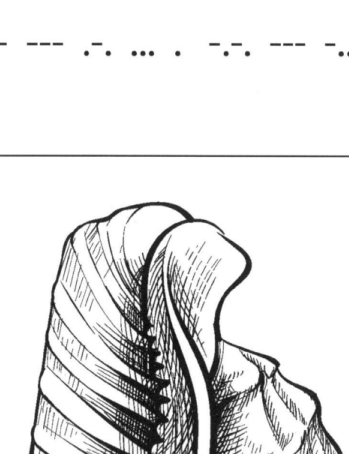

A .-	B -...	C -.-.	D -..
E .	F ..-.	G --.	H ....
I ..	J .---	K -.-	L .-..
M --	N -.	O ---	P .--.
Q --.-	R .-.	S ...	T -
U ..-	V ...-	W .--	X -..-
Y -.--	Z --..	0 -----	1 .----
2 ..---	3 ...--	4 ....-	5 .....
6 -....	7 --...	8 ---..	9 ----.

All rights reserved www.KrakenSky.com

MAKE YOUR OWN SECRET CODE! Making up a code is easy!

1. Create a symbol for each letter in the top alphabet. Be sure they are all different!

Your Copy:

A	B	C	D	E	F	G	H	I	J	K	L	M

N	O	P	Q	R	S	T	U	V	W	X	Y	Z

 2. Now make a copy of the EXACT same code as you used above.

3. Cut along the dotted line, and give this part of the page to your friend!

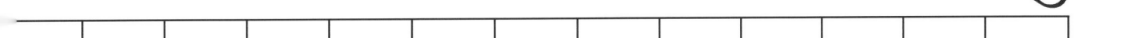

A	B	C	D	E	F	G	H	I	J	K	L	M

N	O	P	Q	R	S	T	U	V	W	X	Y	Z

All rights reserved www.KrakenSky.com

MAKE YOUR OWN SECRET CODE! Making up a code is easy!

Tip: Using graph paper or squares makes it easier to keep the symbols all the same size

Put your code in the gray squares ⇨

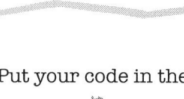

Leave the white squares empty for your friend to write the decoded message ⇨

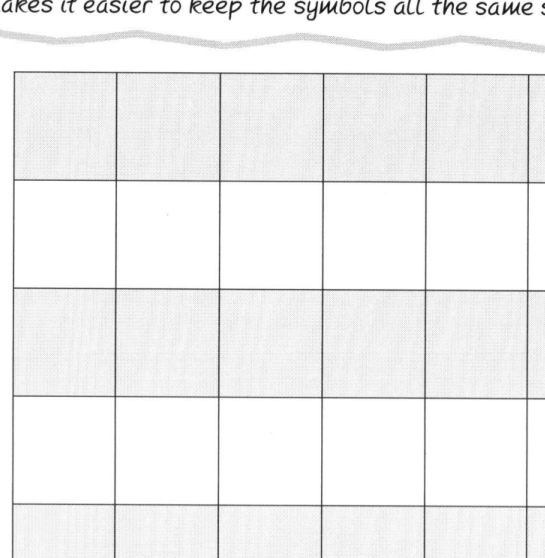

If you have a space between words, leave an empty block to make it easier to decode

Here is an example:

The part you pass back and forth ⇨

The Decoder Alphabet ⇩

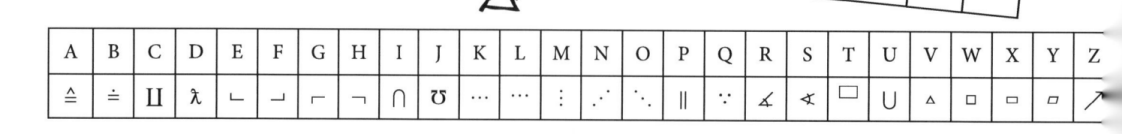

A	B	C	D	E	F	G	H	I	J	K	L	M	N	O	P	Q	R	S	T	U	V	W	X	Y	Z
≙	≐	Π	λ	∟	⌐	⌐	¬	∩	℧	···	···	∶	.·	∵	∥	∵	∠	◁	□	∪	△	◻	◻	◻	╱

All rights reserved www.KrakenSky.com

EASY TWO-ROPE KNOTS

How much rope would you need to sail a pirate ship?

Here's an example: The Queen Anne's Revenge was a ship from the early 1700s, best own as the main hip of the pirate Blackbeard.

ship like Queen Anne's Revenge needed about 43 miles of rope, which weighed round 78.5 tons.

s a comparison, 3 miles of rope uld loop around football field 760 times and be as heavy as large military tank!

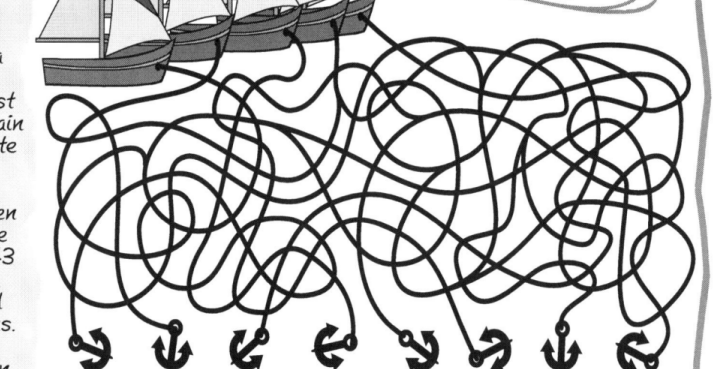

Can you untangle the anchors?

#DYK

In sailing, a nautical mile is a special way to measure distance on water.

One nautical mile is a little longer than a regular mile on land—it's about 1.15 land miles.

A long time ago, sailors used a method called "knots" to measure how fast their ship was moving.

They used a tool called a "common log," which was a rope with knots tied in it, and a piece of wood shaped like a slice of pie.

They would throw the wood into the water behind the ship and let the rope run out for a set time. Then they would count the knots on the rope to see how fast the ship was going.

The speed of the ship was the number of knots they counted.

I tried to tell a rope joke, but it was a "tangle" of words...

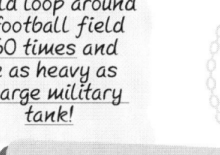

Granny Knot

The granny knot is used to tie a rope around something to keep it secure. It is said to have gotten its name because it was often used to tie sacks in places called granaries where grain was stored.

Square Knot

One of the simplest knots is the square knot. This knot is great for tying things together, like bundles of sticks or gear.

It's also used in first aid to tie a bandage around a cut to stop the bleeding quickly.

Sheet Bend Knot

Handy for joining ropes that have different thicknesses or stiffness. Plus, it's quick and easy to tie!

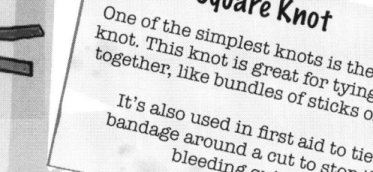

Fisherman's Knot

The fisherman's knot also called the anchor bend, is a very strong and simple knot. It won't get stuck or slip when pulled tight and can be untied easily.

This knot is used to tie a rope to a ring, hook, anchor, or other object.

All rights & permissions: Www.KrakenSky.com

WEATHER CROSSWORD

Across:

7. Height above Mean Sea Level
9. A luminous arc featuring all colors of the visible light spectrum.
10. The record and description of average daily and in seasonal weather events.
11. Used for measuring temperature.
15. A type of humidity that considers the mass of water vapor present per unit volume of space.
17. A subjective term for warm and humid weather.
18. Any and all forms of water, liquid or solid, that falls from clouds
21. Rising and falling of the earth's oceans.
23. Season of the year as the sun approaches the summer solstice.
24. The center of a tropical storm or hurricane.

Down:

1. A nautical unit of speed.
2. Light cloud layer.
3. A forecast issued when severe weather has developed, is already occurring and reported, or is detected on radar.
4. The name for a tropical cyclone.
5. A horizontal movement of water.
6. High water flow or an overflow of rivers or streams.
8. Abnormal dry weather for a specific area.
12. Lightning that appears as a glowing flash on the horizon.
13. The process by which water vapor undergoes a change in state from a gas to a liquid.
14. The physical process by which a liquid, such as water, is transformed into a gas.
16. A measure of temperature difference
19. The sound emitted by rapidly expanding gases along the channel of a lightning discharge.
20. A slang term used in the United States for a tornado.
22. Air that flows in relation to the earth's surface, generally horizontally.

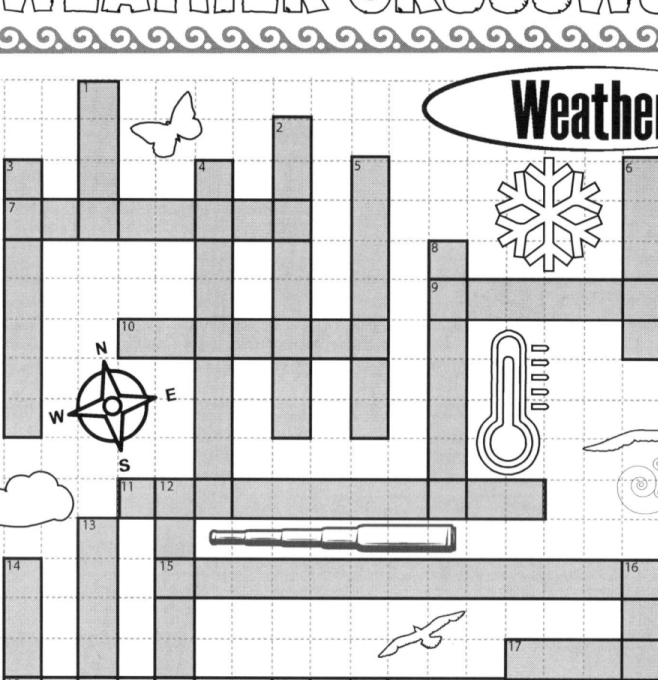

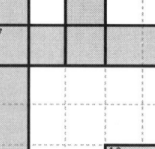 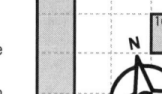    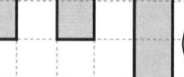 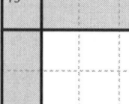  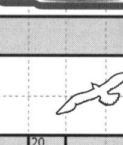

Word Bank

WIND – DROUGHT – ALTITUDE – HUMIDITY – PRECIPITATION – FLOOD – OVERCAST – TWISTER – EVAPORATION – RAINBOW – CLIMATE – KNOT – WARNING – CONDENSATION – DEGREE – MUGGY – HURRICANE – THERMOMETER – TIDE – SPRING – THUNDER – HEAT LIGHTNING – CURRENT – EYE

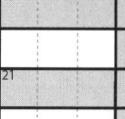 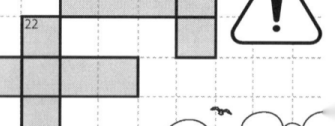

At the beach or pool and hear thunder or see lightning? Get out of the water! Electrical charges travel across the surface over great distances when lightning hits the water.

Wait 30 minutes or more after the storm passes before heading back to the beach.

All rights & permissions: Www.KrakenSky.com

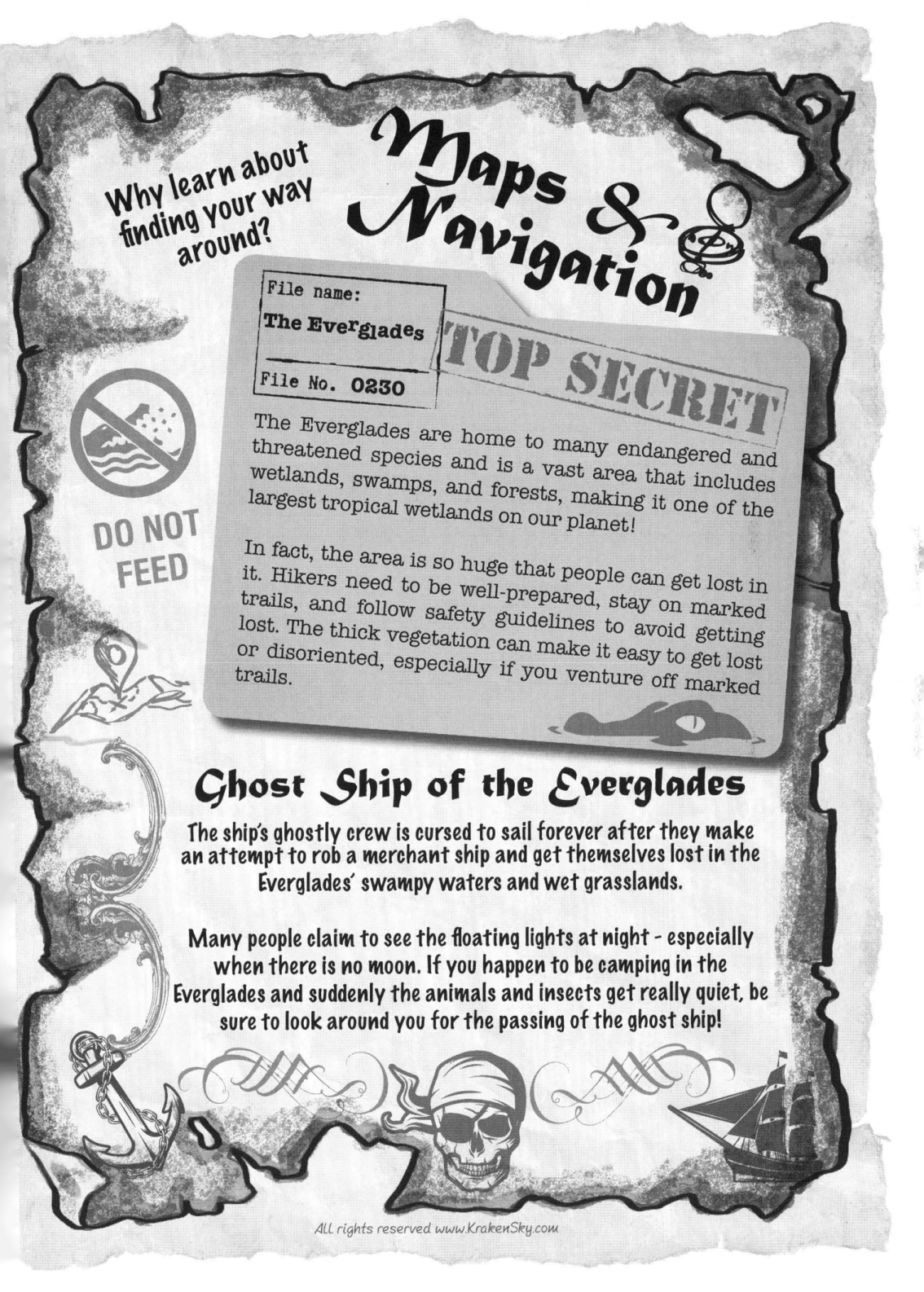

SUNKEN TREASURE

The Nuestra Señora de Atocha

A Lost Spanish Treasure Galleon!

The Atocha made the Guinness Book of World Records for being the most valuable shipwreck ever to be recovered!

It's been said that 40 tons of gold and silver, and 71 pounds of emeralds sank with the Atocha!

The Nuestra Señora de Atocha was a Spanish treasure galleon that went down in a storm, way back in 1622.

It ended up on the sea floor under 56 ft of water between Key West, FL, and Havana, Cuba.

That depth made it very hard for divers in that era to bring back up anything of value from the ship.

Then, a second hurricane a month later scattered the wreckage of the sunken ship over an even wider area.

In perspective...

70 Pounds = 1 Bag of Concrete Mix

1 Ton = 2,000 pounds, worth approximately (today) $55 million

40 Tons = 11 adult hippos

Most of the treasure was found by commercial treasure hunter, Mel Fisher, and his family in the 1970's. However, due to that second storm - and so many since then - pieces of the ship and it's belongings are still being found to this day...

Much more info at www.melfisher.com

All rights & permissions: Www.KrakenSky.com

Reading a COMPASS

The four **cardinal** directions are north (N), east (E), south (S), west (W), at $90°$ angles.

The four **intercardinal** directions are in the middle of those are northeast (NE), southeast (SE), southwest (SW), and northwest (NW).

Word Scramble

RTNOH

_____

HSTOU

_____

ETAS

_____

SWET

_____

Can you fill in the missing cardinal directions?

Now fill in the intercardinal directions!

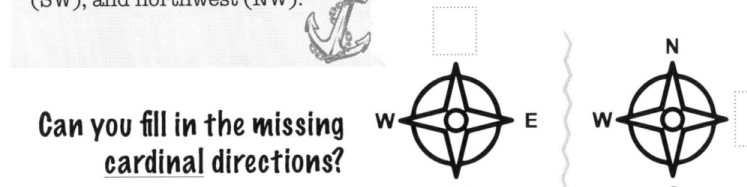

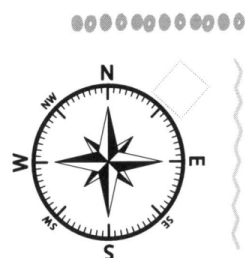

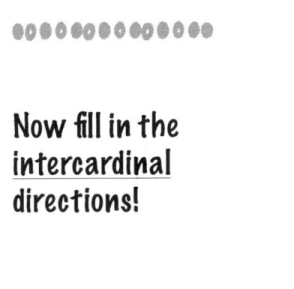

All rights & permissions: Www.KrakenSky.com

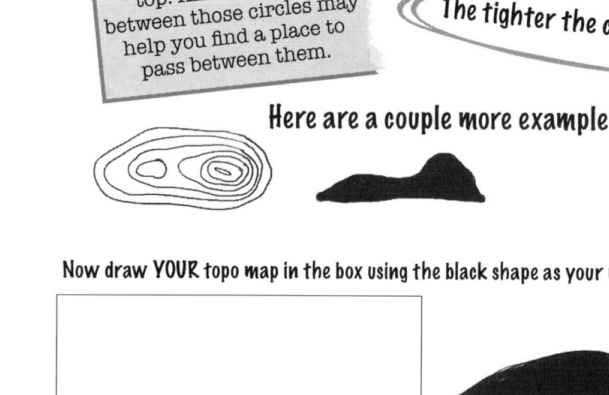
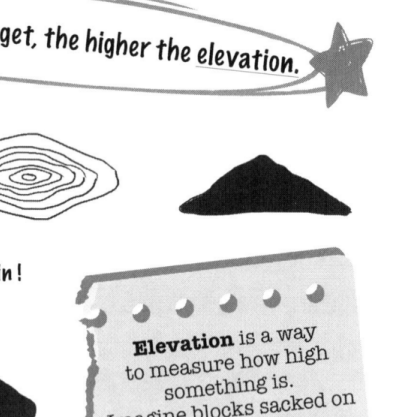
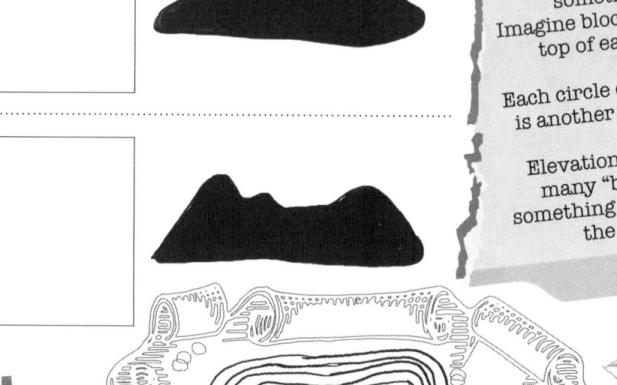

WORD SCRAMBLE & SEARCH

Find and unscramble the boating terms below

S	Q	V	Q	E	O	E	E	L	E	J	G	M	Z
I	X	X	X	F	M	C	S	E	B	H	M	N	V
J	U	M	X	C	X	C	J	E	R	O	Q	G	Q
W	X	S	K	K	F	N	B	W	Z	Q	W	R	W
X	P	R	T	Q	J	F	K	A	C	S	B	W	I
O	Y	B	U	A	D	H	U	R	Y	Y	O	P	N
I	A	P	L	D	R	Q	R	D	W	R	O	P	D
P	U	S	O	X	D	B	M	P	C	E	M	O	W
E	J	H	N	R	O	E	O	C	D	J	K	S	A
S	G	X	O	V	T	K	R	A	D	E	W	T	R
J	I	B	I	N	G	E	Z	C	R	W	Z	W	D
A	F	T	K	N	G	H	I	V	D	D	E	V	Q
N	L	F	P	S	H	Z	T	A	C	K	I	N	G

WDIWARN _____

TBRRODASA _____

EWLRDAE _____

UREDRD _____

TAF _____

RTPO _____

NKGICAT _____

WOB _____

IIGJBN _____

BOMO _____

Aft - The back of the boat. Aft is also sometimes called the stern.

Bow - The front of the boat.

Port - When facing the bow, the Port side is the left-hand side of the boat.

Starboard - The right-hand side of the boat when facing the bow (front).

Leeward - (Or lee) is opposite to the direction the wind is blowing (windward).

Windward - The direction the wind blows or moving with the wind.

Boom - Big horizontal pole at the bottom of the mast.

Rudder - Under the boat, the rudder is a flat piece of construction used to steer the ship.

Tacking - Turning the front of the boat through the wind to go in the other direction.

Jibing - Turning the back of the boat through the wind to change the boat's course.

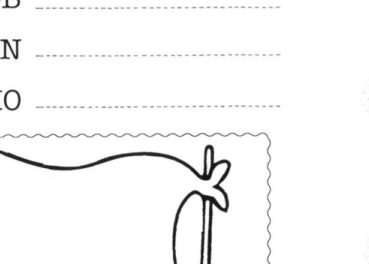

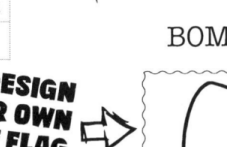

#DYK September 19 every year is International Talk Like a Pirate Day!

Arrr, Arrgh, Yarr, Gar - Pirate for "whatever", "got it", etc...

Heave - Come to a stop.

Avast – "Focus!"

Davy Jones's Locker – Undersea land of monsters and ghosts.

Parley - A compromise or agreement.

Ahoy – "Hello" or "What's up?"

Prize – Something valuable to be stolen.

Aye – "Yes"

Weigh Anchor – "Get going!"

Matey – Friends of pirates.

Shiver Me Timbers – A shock or surprise!

All rights & permissions: Www.KrakenSky.com

THE ZODIAC CONSTELLATIONS
Ancient Calendar in the Stars

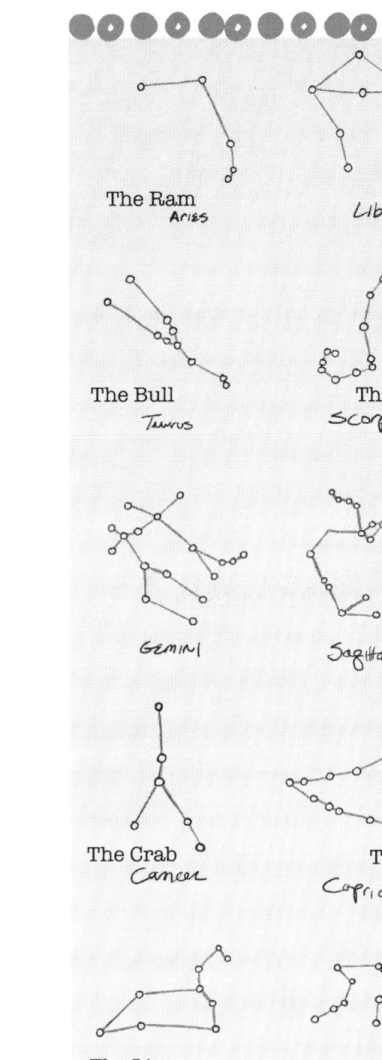

What is the Zodiac?
There are 12 constellations in the zodiac family, each standing for a unit of time, equal to about a month.

These were used as an ancient calendar because the sun would pass through the constellations in the same order, at the same pace, every year.

#DYK
"Zodiac" means "circle of animals" in Greek, chosen because seven of the constellations are thought to look like animals.

Aries	March 21 - April 19
Taurus	April 20 - May 20
Gemini	May 21 - June 20
Cancer	June 21 - July 22
Leo	July 23 - August 22
Virgo	August 23 - September 22
Libra	September 23 - October 22
Scorpio	October 23 - November 21
Sagittarius	November 22 - December 21
Capricorn	December 22 - January 19
Aquarius	January 20 - February 18
Pisces	February 19 - March 20

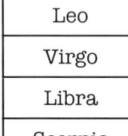

So you would be looking for what constellation in the sky if...

1. You needed to leave port by May 1st in order to have enough time to sail home for your best friend's birthday?

2. You had to start planting crops on March 1st?

3. You were going on your first big expedition on October 30th?

All rights & permissions: www.KrakenSky.com

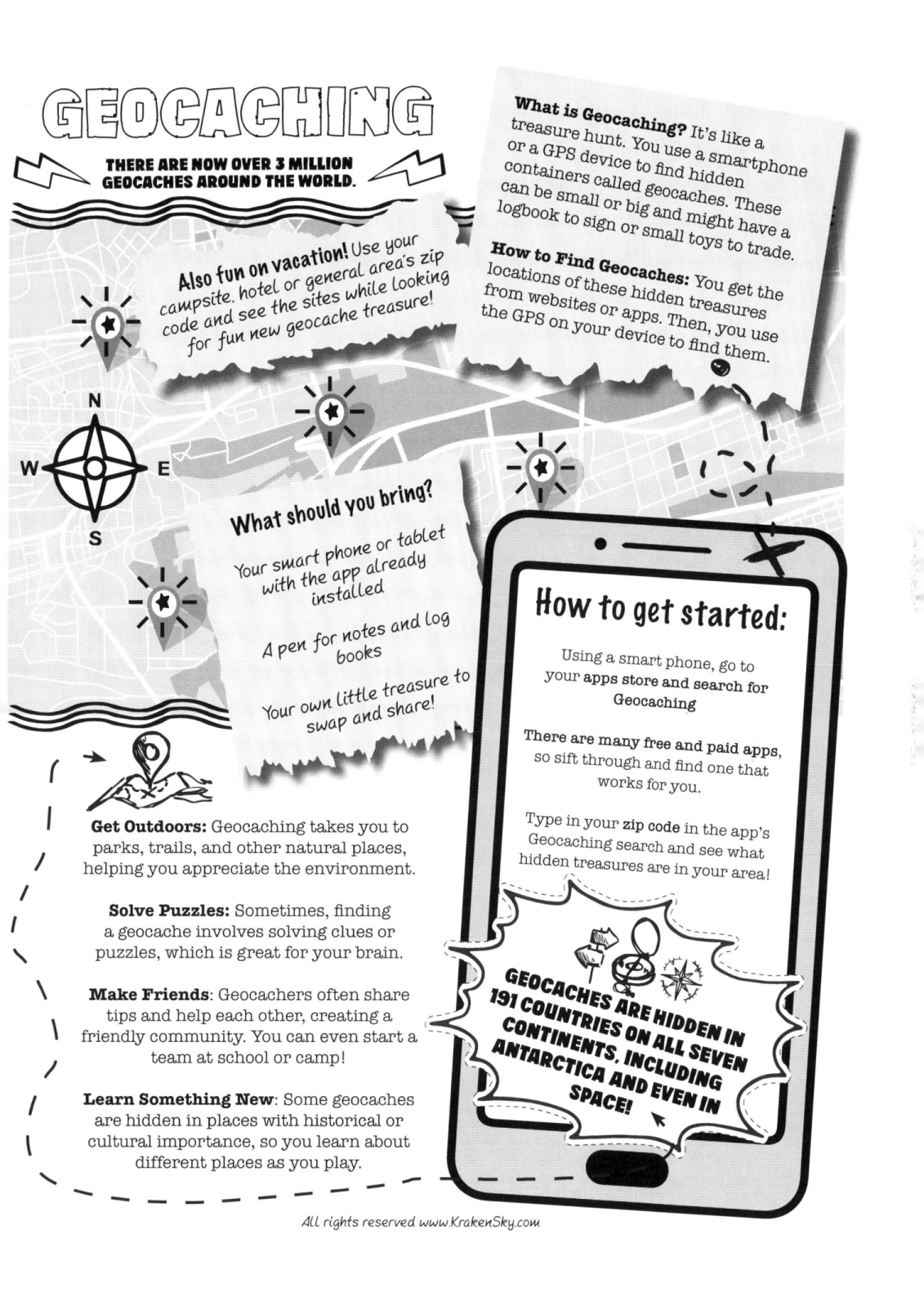

Pirate News

VOL 12345 **shipwreck journal** NO 123

The 1715 Treasure Fleet

The 1715 Treasure Fleet was made up of two Spanish treasure fleets coming back from the New World to Spain: the "Nueva España Fleet" and the "Tierra Firme Fleet".

Early in the morning on July 31, 1715, all eleven ships in the fleet were caught in a hurricane and sank along the east coast of Florida.

The fleet was carrying a lot of silver, so it's also called the 1715 Plate Fleet (plata is the Spanish word for silver).

It took 200 years before the shipwreck was found again. In 1928, William J. Beach discovered the remains of the Urca de Lima near Fort Pierce. People started searching for treasure there in 1932, with more attempts in 1983 and 1984.

They found a silver bar, some cannons, and two silver pieces!

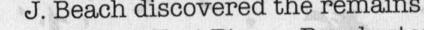

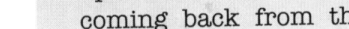

Today's Pirate Horoscope:

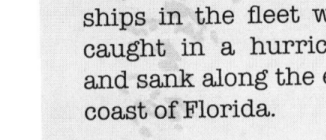

Daily Pirating Tips

Silver bars weigh about 6.86 pounds each, so they are easy to handle. Most 100-ounce silver bars are very pure, almost 100% silver.

This means you can stash lots of loot in a small space!

Crazy Harry's Compass Cleaning

**Repairs & Cleaning Services
44 Dockside Drive**

Just look for the hook marks around the door handle!

"Who knows! We might even give it back!"

All rights reserved www.KrakenSky.com

More Treasure Found

July 31, 2015- Brent Brisbon and his company, Queens Jewels, LLC, discovered $4.5 million worth of gold coins off the Florida coast. These coins were part of the 1715 Spanish Treasure Fleet. They found nine "Royals," special coins made for King Philip V of Spain, worth $300,000 each.

The artifacts, which were only about 15 feet deep in the water, included 51 gold coins and 40 feet of ornate gold chain.

Since the ship was found over fifty years ago, divers have found about $50 million worth of treasure. They believe there could still be more than $400 million worth of treasure hidden under the sea.

$1 million worth of gold in the shallow waters about 30 miles north of West Palm Beach!

In 2015, it was estimated that there could still be $400 million worth of treasure from the 1715 shipwrecks on the ocean floor!

Still Looking?

Now, the wreck site is an underwater preserve, and is listed on the National Register of Historic Places.

Sometimes, pieces of the treasure still wash up on Florida beaches...

$4.5 million worth of gold coins off the Florida coast.

All rights reserved www.KrakenSky.com

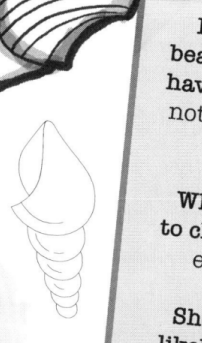
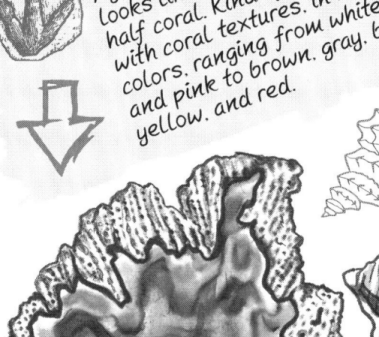

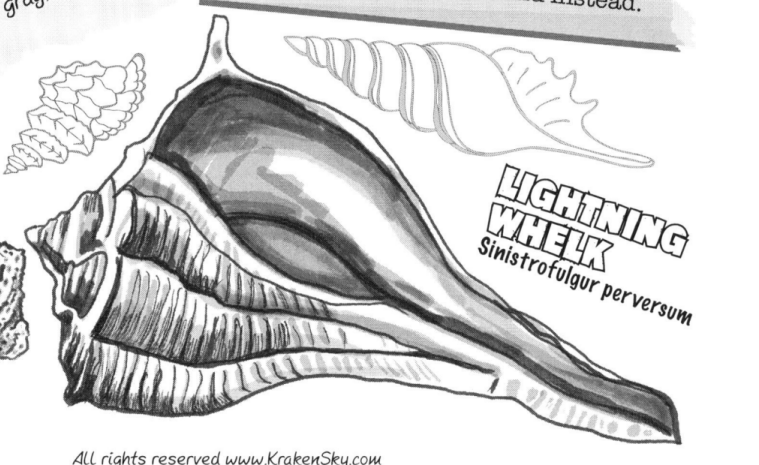

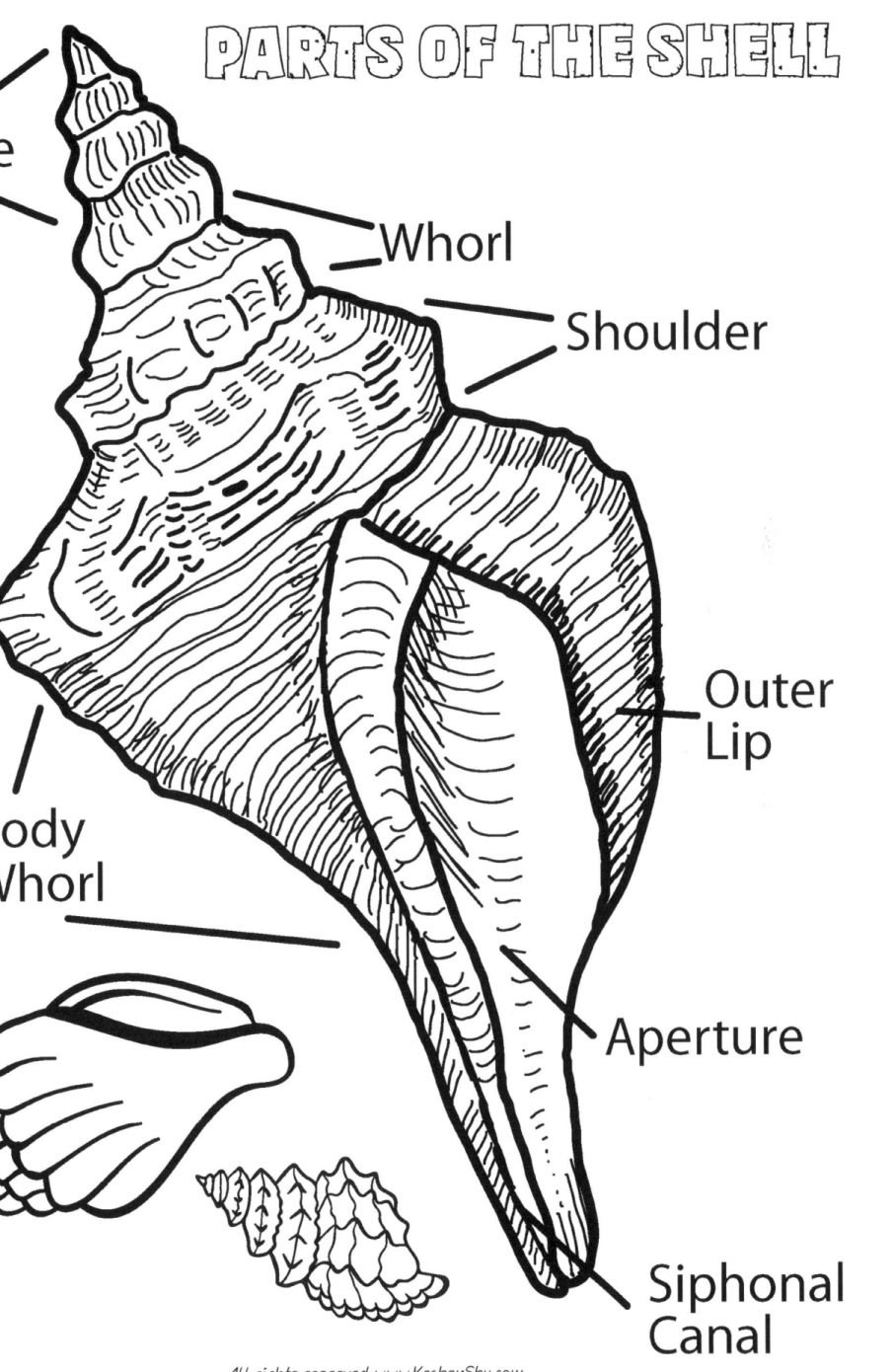

BEACH TRIP - Scavenger Hunt & Connect Four

Player Name:_____ Date:_____ Score:_____

Player Name:_____ Date:_____ Score:_____

Player Name:_____ Date:_____ Score:_____

Player Name:_____ Date:_____ Score:_____

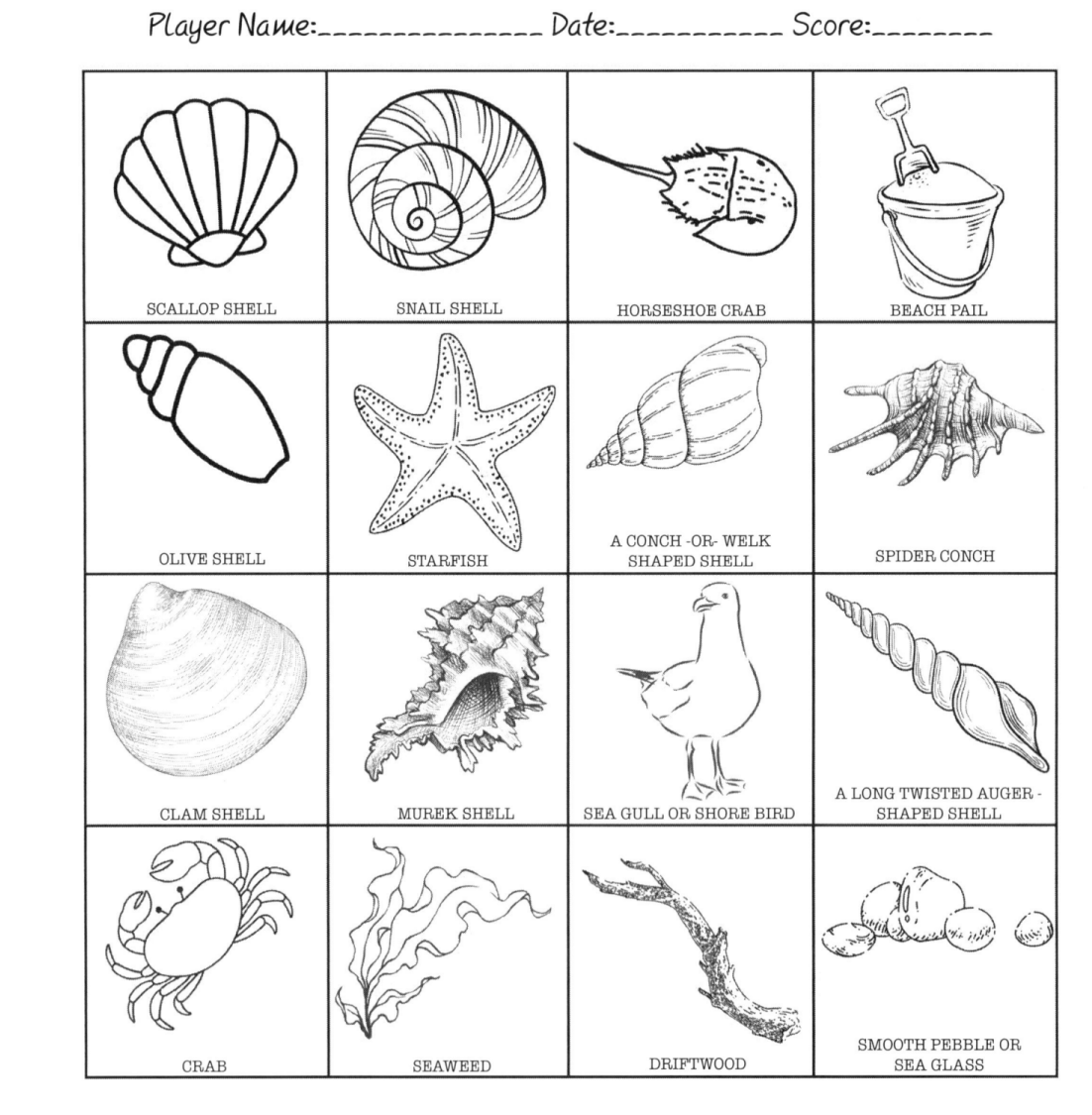

Connect 4 in a row -or- get 1 point for every found object!

Check off or write the player's initials each box when found to keep score.

All rights reserved www.KrakenSky.com

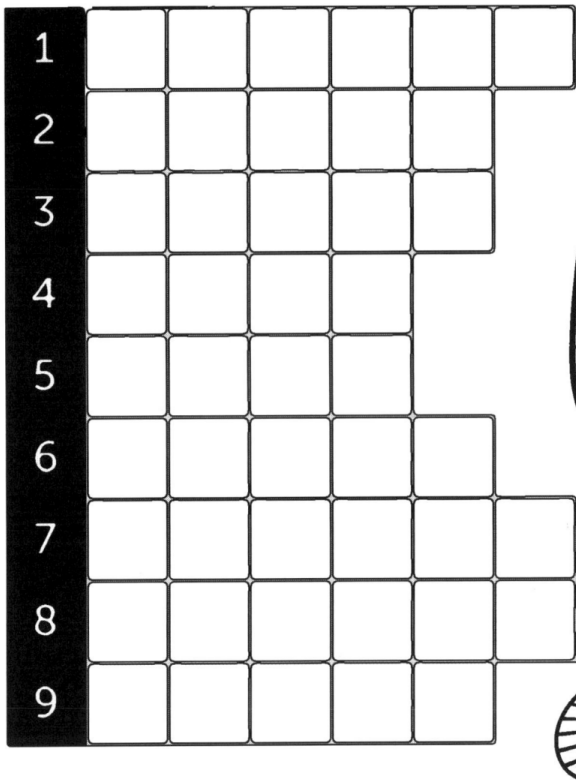

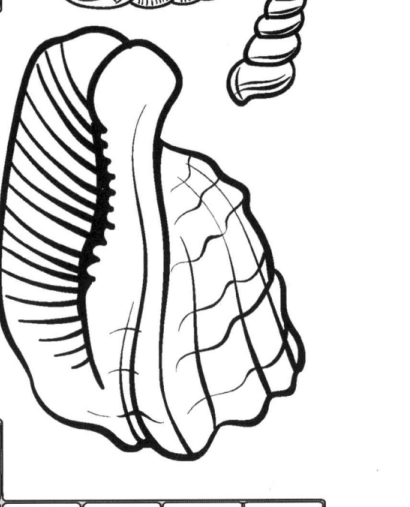

Scrambles

1. mtLiep
2. SaIni
3. klheW
4. onCe
5. atrS
6. Mrxue
7. eystOr
8. ilPiewrnke
9. hcoCn

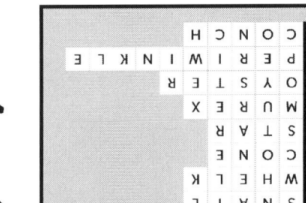

All rights reserved www.KrakenSky.com

WOODLAND TRAIL - Scavenger Hunt & Connect Four

Player Name:_____ Date:_____ Score:_____

Player Name:_____ Date:_____ Score:_____

Player Name:_____ Date:_____ Score:_____

Player Name:_____ Date:_____ Score:_____

Connect 4 in a row -or- get 1 point for every found object!

Check off or write the player's initials each box when found to keep score.

All rights reserved www.KrakenSky.com

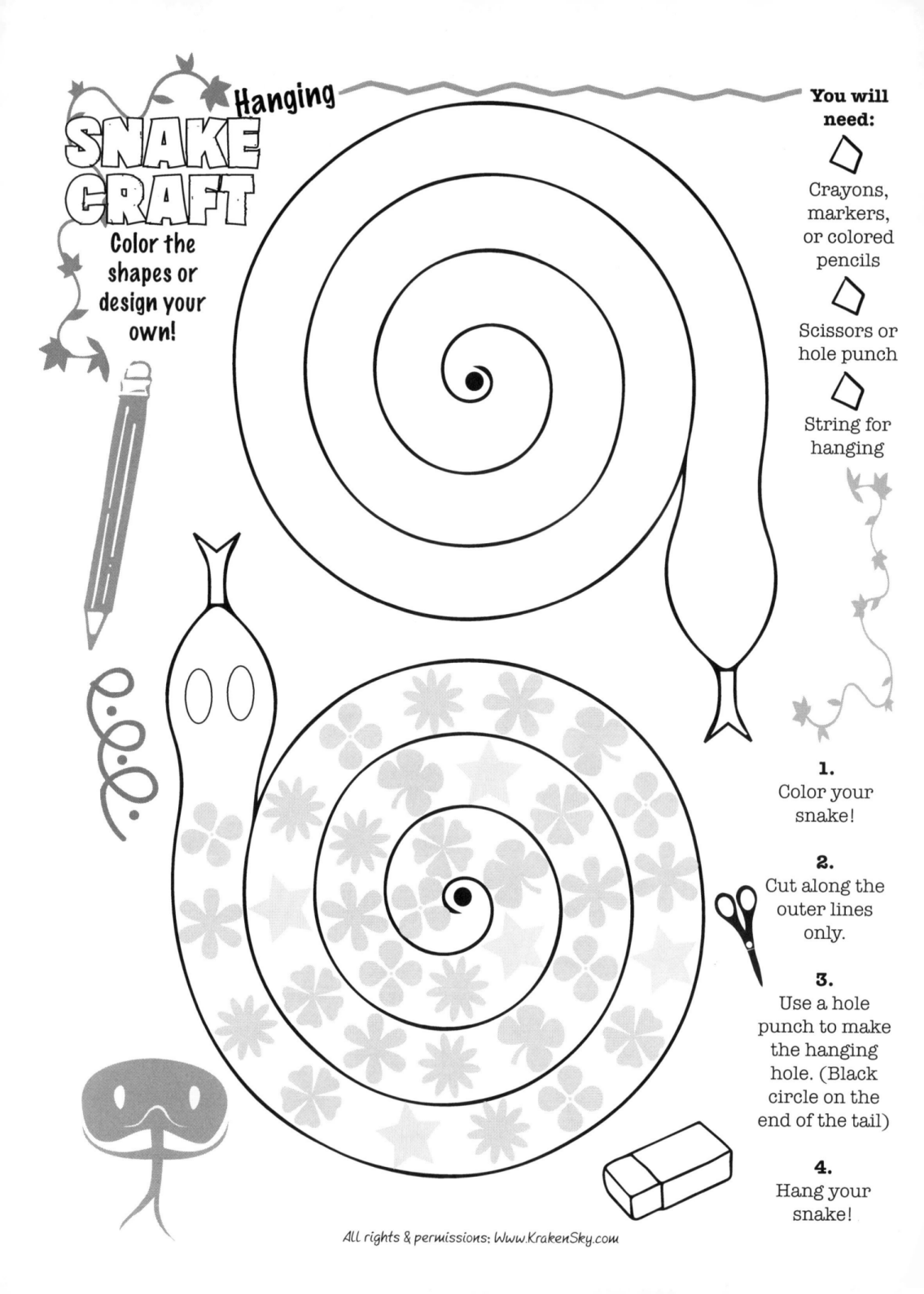

DRIFTWOOD CRAFTS

Hanging Decorations

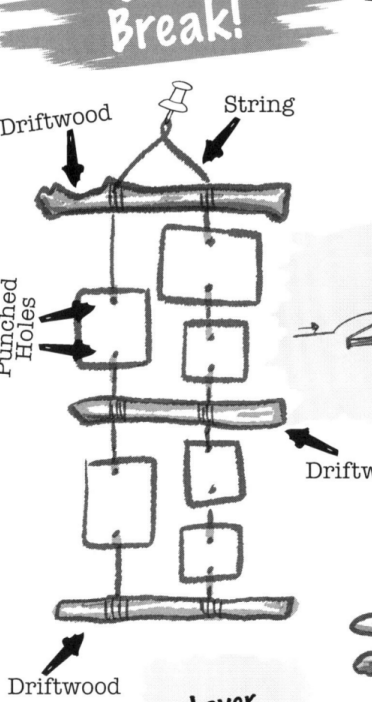

✓ **Prep:** Soaking or boiling driftwood will help to kill off any spores or bacteria from the beach.

Attaching Pictures

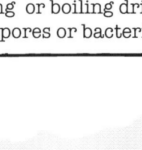

Stringing any flat items like the diagram shown lets you keep the string from covering your picture.

Layer number optional!

Materials:

String & Scissors (or wire, yarn, twine, etc.)

Driftwood

Pictures (or cards, handmade paper, fabric, etc.)

Hole Punch

Optional: Paint, bells, beads, ornaments, shells, etc.

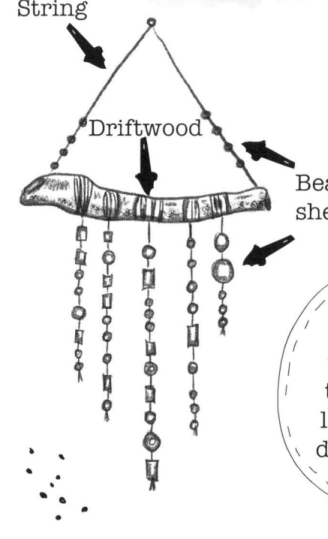

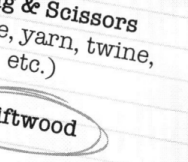

Wrapping and tying the string to the driftwood lets you skip any drilling or gluing!

PRO TIPS

Put knots on either sides of your ornaments to create more space or keep them in place.

All rights & permissions: Www.KrakenSky.com

Which of these shapes only shows up once?

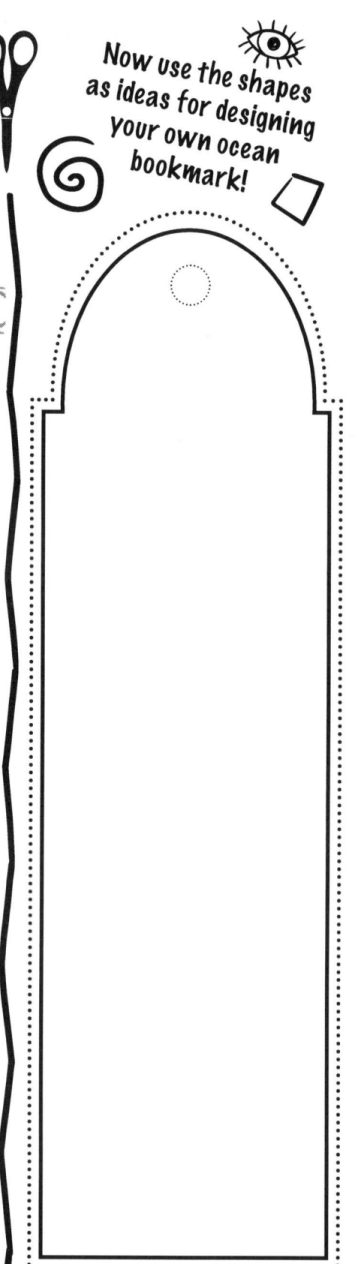

Now use the shapes as ideas for designing your own ocean bookmark!

Cut along the dotted line and use a hole punch to add a ribbon or yarn!

All rights & permissions: Www.KrakenSky.com

Prep: Soaking or boiling driftwood will help to kill off any spores or bacteria from the beach.

DRIFTWOOD CRAFTS
Driftwood Monsters!

You Need:
Driftwood!
+

Optional:
Paint, bells, beads, ornaments, shells, markers, glitter glue, pipe cleaners, feathers, google eyes, plastic gems, felt, found objects, etc.

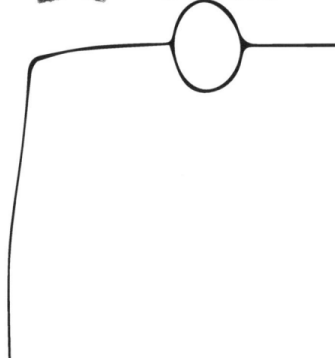

Use the blank spaces to sketch out ideas!

All rights & permissions: Www.KrakenSky.com

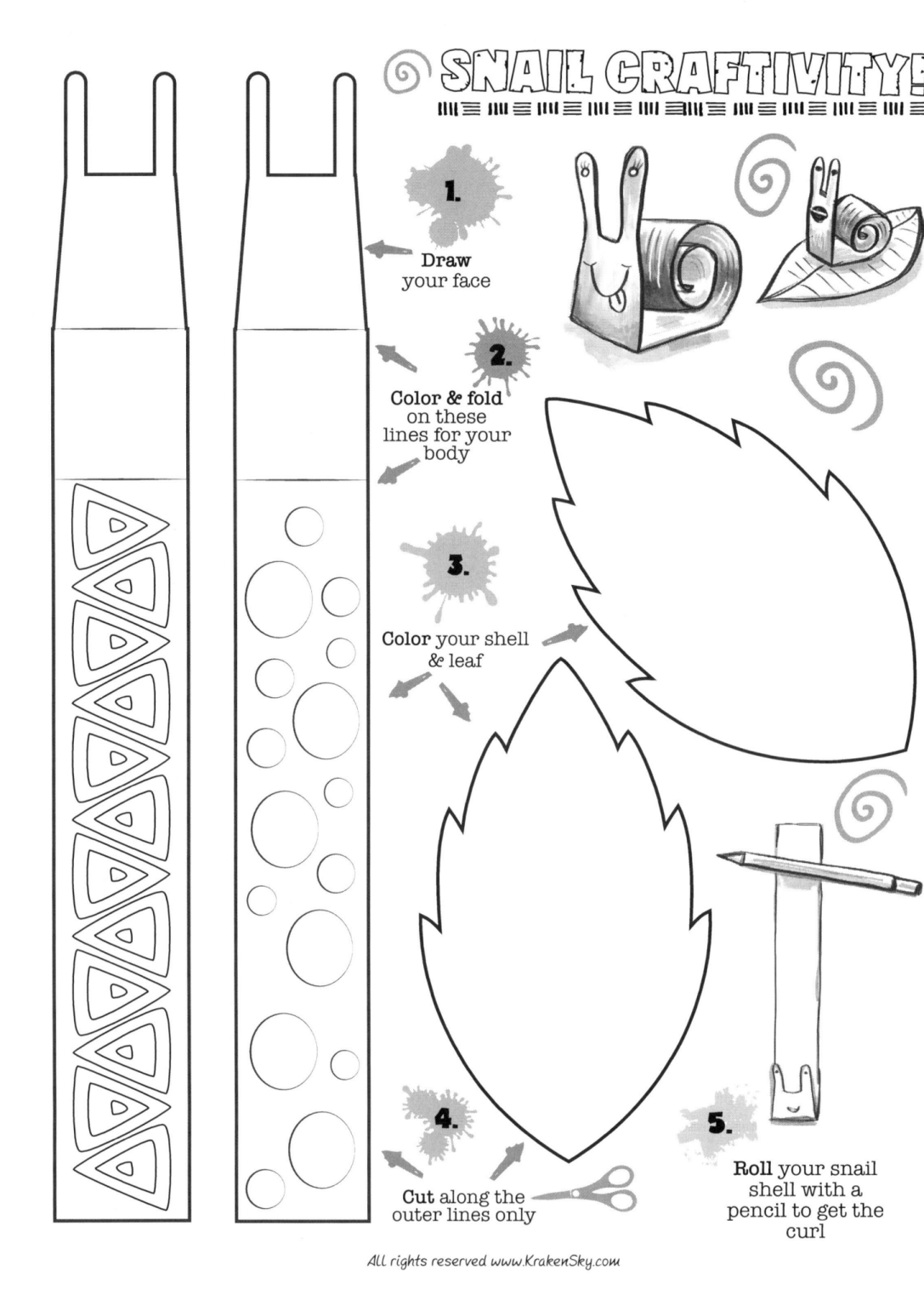

SNAIL MAD LIBS

Mesomphix globosus

Step 1. Ask a friend for the following words, but don't tell them why!

Step 2. Add them -in order- to the story Snails Are So Cool.

Step 3. Read the story to them with their words in the sentences!

Snails have more teeth than any other animal!

A garden snail has about 14,000 teeth, and some other kinds of snails can have over 20,000 teeth.

But the most amazing thing is that the teeth of a water snail called the limpet are the strongest material made by any living creature, even stronger than titanium!

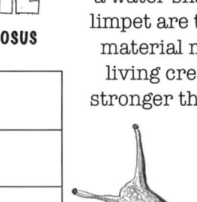

A Color:	
An Adjective:	
A Time:	
An Adjective:	
A Place:	
A Food:	
A Food:	
A Verb:	
A Person:	
A Number:	

Adjectives *are words that describe what something is like, such as enormous, dog-like, silly, yellow, fun, or fast.*

Verbs *are words that show actions. These actions can be things we do on the outside (like run, jump, work) or things we do on the inside (like love, think, or consider).*

Snails Are So Cool!

They are_____, _____ creatures.

They like to crawl around at_____which makes some people think they are gross.

But snails are_____, and wouldn't hurt anyone.

I know a snail that lives at _____.

I like to feed him _____and _____.

He likes to_____.

I am his favorite person, but he also likes _____.

I want to make friends with _____ more snails.

All rights & permissions: Www.KrakenSky.com

Word Search

H	K	M	R	O	W	C	A	D	I	R	O	L	F	L
V	W	N	B	L	E	I	T	S	X	S	A	S	C	S
C	J	U	E	B	S	T	X	I	N	W	C	S	T	P
M	J	Z	A	U	S	N	N	A	R	R	Q	A	Y	E
C	B	L	U	T	C	A	I	I	A	B	R	R	C	A
A	V	L	T	T	U	L	U	S	R	R	A	G	H	R
N	X	I	I	O	L	T	S	Y	O	E	T	C	E	C
T	E	R	F	N	P	A	A	W	C	T	U	H	S	O
H	R	D	U	Q	T	B	D	X	K	S	R	T	T	S
A	U	G	L	E	U	N	D	E	W	Y	B	O	N	T
R	M	U	L	Y	R	N	R	I	B	O	A	O	U	A
U	G	L	K	L	E	H	H	O	C	B	N	M	T	T
S	A	F	P	D	D	W	P	R	H	A	I	S	G	E
G	N	I	N	T	H	G	I	L	X	I	L	R	X	T
P	O	T	E	L	K	N	I	W	I	R	E	P	Y	Q

ATLANTIC · MUREX
BAY · OYSTER
BEAUTIFUL · PEAR
BUTTON · PERIWINKLE
CABRIT · PLACID
CANTHARUS · RIBBED
CHESTNUT · ROCK
COSTATE · SCULPTURED
CRASSATELLA · SMOOTH
DRILL · SNAIL
FLORIDA · STAR
GRASS · TOP
GULF · TURBAN
HORN · WORM
LIGHTNING

All rights reserved www.KrakenSky.com

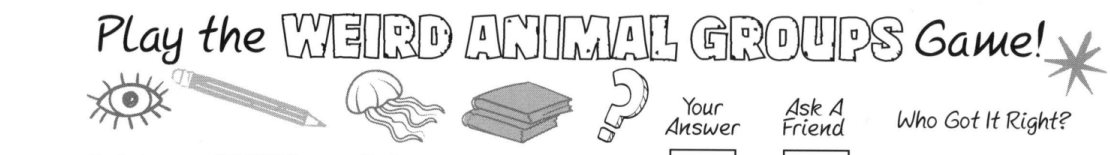

Play the WEIRD ANIMAL GROUPS Game!

	Your Answer	Ask A Friend	Who Got It Right?

1. A group of FOXES are called:
A. A Wiggle, B. A Leash, C. A Pod, D. A Knot

2. A group of FROGS are called:
A. A Drool, B. An Orchestra, C. An Army, D. A Boat

3. A group of GIRAFFES are called:
A. A Tower, B. An Envelope, C. A Corporation, D. a Tally

4. A group of JELLYFISH are called:
A. A Sneeze, B. A Dance, C. A Smack, D. A Fortress

5. A group of WOMBATS are called:
A. A Welt, B. A Wall, C. A Circle, D. A Wisdom

6. A group of ELEPHANTS are called (besides herd):
A. A Burst, B. A Parade, C. A Club, D. A Mosh

7. A group of ELK are called:
A. A Gang, B. A Bluster, C. A Pocket, D. A Rush

8. A group of BATS are called:
A. A Bucket, B. A Blather, C. A Colony, D. A Hocus

9. A group of ALLIGATORS are called:
A. A Forrest, B. A Foam, C. A Mess, D. A Congregation

10. A group of RHINOCEROSES are called:
A. A Crash, B. A Party, C. A Riot, D. A Stone

11. A group of FERRETS are called:
A. A Bundle, B. A Business, C. A Cuddle, D. A Cache

12. A group of CROWS are called:
A. A Celebration, B. A Shop, C. A Murder, D. A Block

13. A group of JAGUARS are called:
A. A Shadow, B. A Moon, C. A Problem, D. A Mellon

14. A group of RAVENS are called:
A. A Mob, B. An Unkindness, C. A Mass, D. An Attack

15. A group of Camels are called:
A. A Chain, B. A Rope, C. A Caravan, D. A Bridge

B 2 C 3 A 4 A 5 C 4 D 5 C 6 B 7 A 8 C 9 D 10 A 11 B 12 C 13 A 14 B 15 C

All rights reserved www.KrakenSky.com

Time to make a TIME CAPSULE

You Need:
Pen
Paper
Air-tight
Glass Jar

Optional:
Photos
Report
Card
Newspaper
Ticket
Stubs
Magazine
Cutouts

Instructions:
Answer some fun questions about yourself!

It is also fun to include photos, cutouts of things you like or enjoy, even the front page of the newspaper!

Seal up the container tight, and write "do not open until....."
(Whatever date you want to wait to revisit your time capsule) on the outside of your time capsule.

Bury, hide or store your capsule somewhere it will be safe until your recovery date!

Name: / Date:

Favorite Songs:

Favorite Books:

Favorite Foods:

Something I wish I already knew how to do:

Something cool I want to accomplish this year:

What I want to be doing in 2 years:

What I want to be doing in 5 years:

Where do I think I want to live as a grown up:

Favorite place to spend time:

All rights reserved www.KrakenSky.com

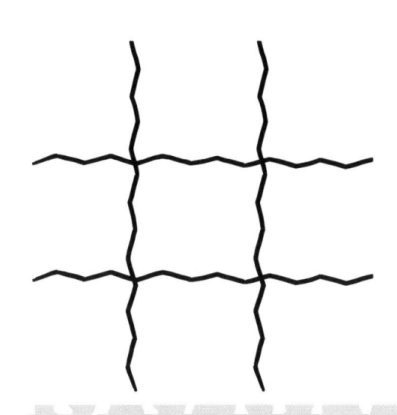

TICK TAC TOE

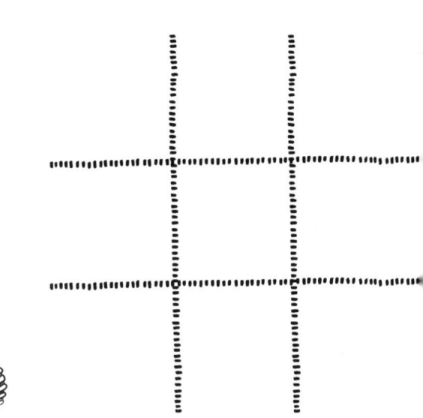

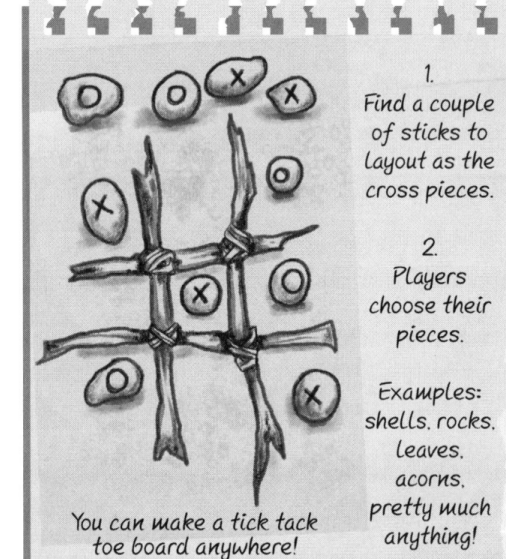

1.
Find a couple of sticks to layout as the cross pieces.

2.
Players choose their pieces.

Examples: shells, rocks, leaves, acorns, pretty much anything!

You can make a tick tack toe board anywhere!

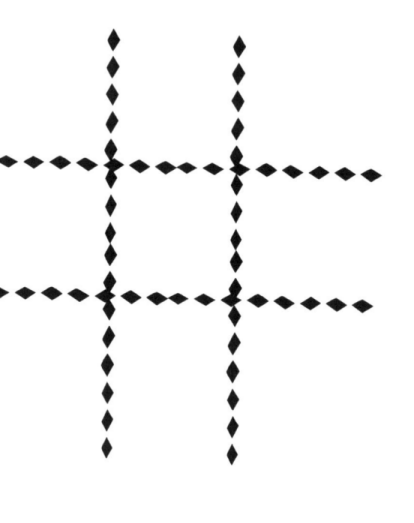

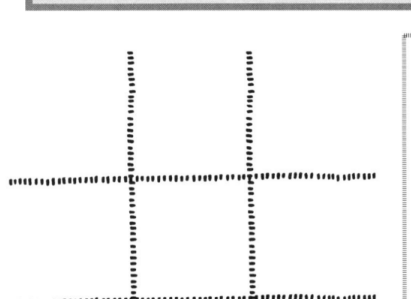

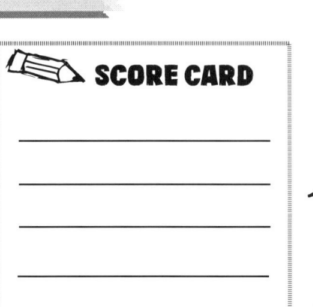

SCORE CARD

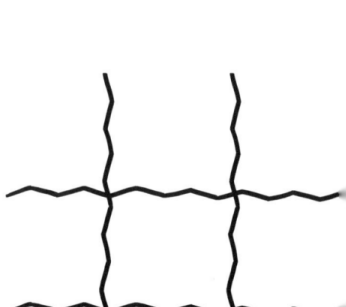

All rights reserved www.KrakenSky.com

First letter of your first name

A - Gussied
B - Elegant
C - Screech
D - Shivers
E - Frilly
F - Peaches
G - Loofah
H - Whistler
I - Heyday
J - Shrimp
K - Flip Flop
L - Mahalo
M - Magnificent
N - Flammy
O - Jelly Bean
P - Pineapple
Q - Poppy
R - Pinky
S - Mango
T - Ruby
U - Tiki
V - Fuego
W - Blush
X - Breezy
Y - Sunny
Z - Pinky

+ The month you were born.... =

January - Shrimperdoodle
February - Noodle-Neckers
March - Sunshinerosa
April - Glimmer-Glammer
May - Walker-Stiltz
June - McFeather-Giggles
July - Feather-Brainerson
August - Beakeroo
September - Snazzy-Sockilla
October - Whisper-Wind
November - LoopyLegz
December - Flufferella

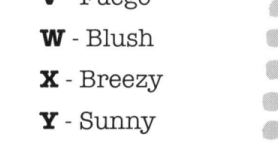

All rights & permissions: Www.KrakenSky.com

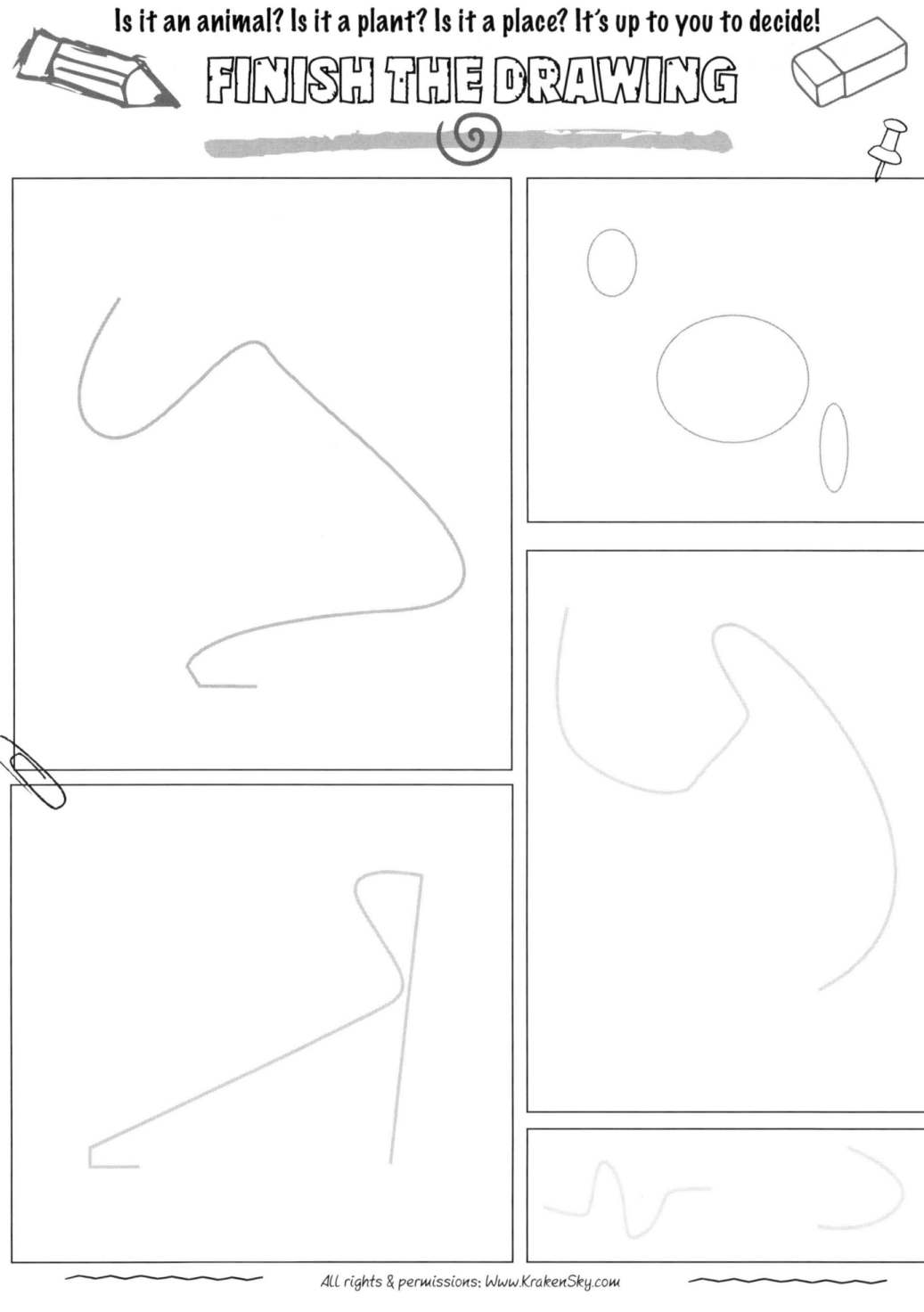

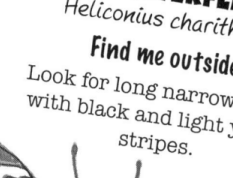

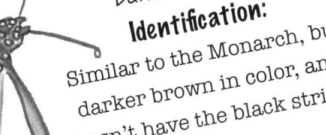

BUTTERFLIES As Art Inspiration! Part Two

Real examples in nature are wonderful to jump start creative ideas!

SPICEBUSH SWALLOWTAIL

Papilio troilus linnaeus

Black with pale blue-green area on lower back and a large orange spot on the middle lowest wing section.

PALAMEDES SWALLOWTAIL OR LAUREL SWALLOWTAIL

Papilio palamedes

Large, dark swallowtail butterfly marked with yellow spots and bands.

HACKBERRY EMPEROR

Asterocampa celtis

Light brown with a row of black or white dots near the far edge of their wings.

CLOUDLESS SULPHUR

Phoebis sennae

Large yellow butterfly with brown spots.

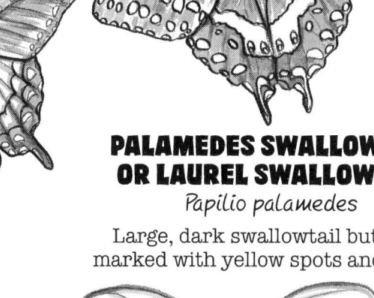

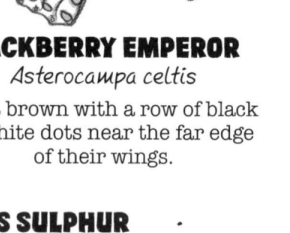

ARE YOU READY? Continuous Line Drawing Challenge!

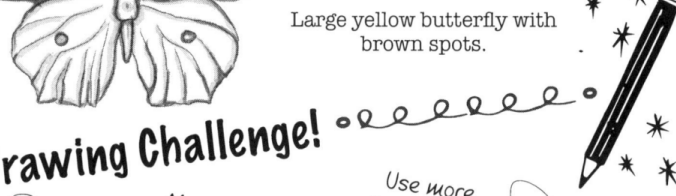

Messy is good!

Use more paper if you need it!

Keep practicing!

Rules:

Don't take your pencil off the page until you finish the drawing!

©

Overlapping is fine!

◇

Fill in the loops with color when you are done!

✿

A **continuous line drawing** is an art exercise where the artist draws an image without taking the pencil off of the page.

All rights reserved www.KrakenSky.com

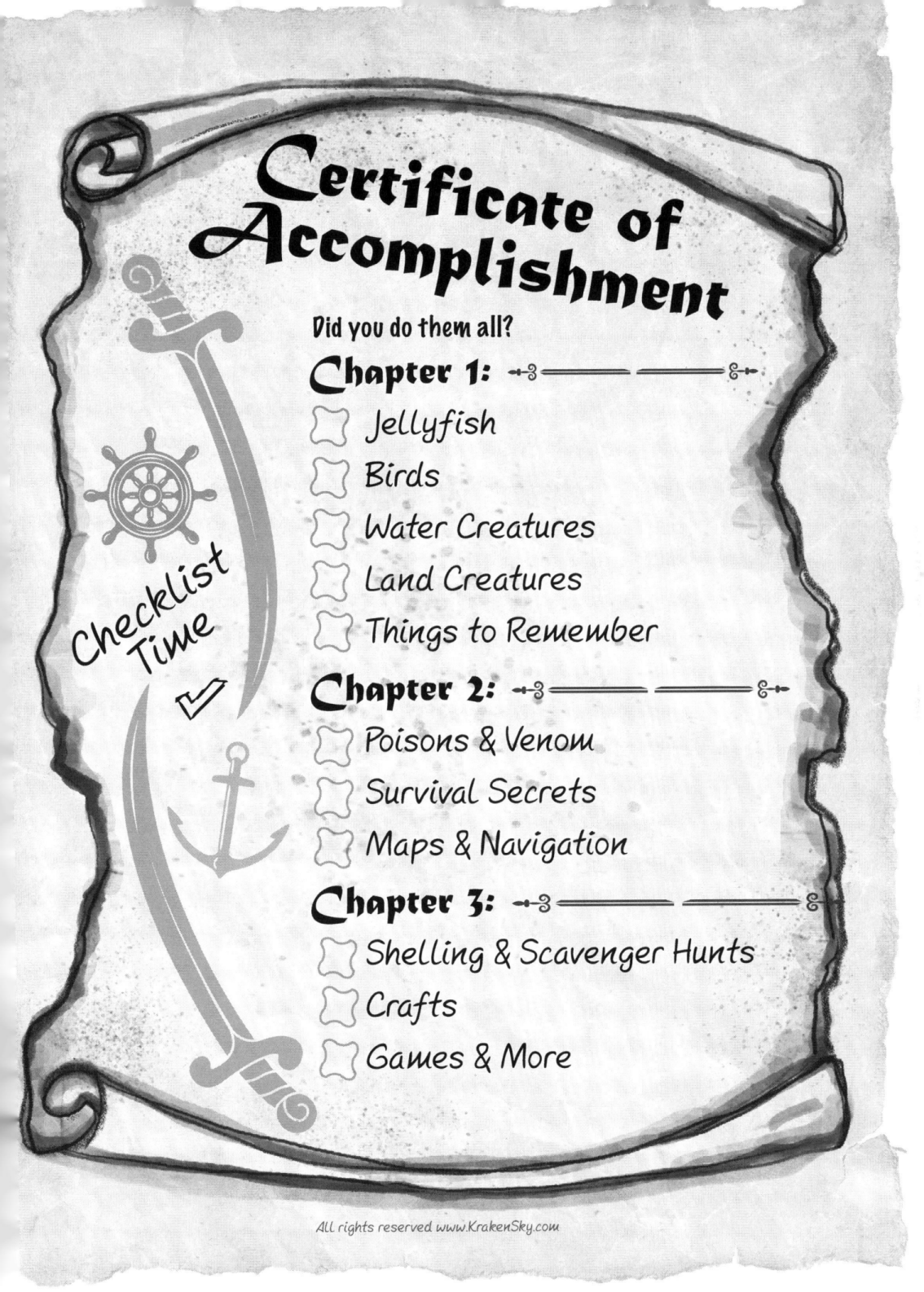

About the Author

website

books on amazon

Julianne Black DiBlasi is the author and illustrator of over two dozen children's books and activity books, including the Augmented Reality enhanced Sleep Sweet, exhibited at Book Expo 2017 in New York City, New York, and is being used nationwide in children's hospitals for relaxation and distraction therapy.

Monthly columnist for Story Monsters Ink Magazine since 2017, an award-winning publication specializing in Children's Literature.

Her work as an internationally recognized and award-winning graphic designer has allowed her the opportunity to work with globally recognized brands for worldwide impact for over 25 years.

Her digital art has been published for multiple years in Comic Con International's Souvenir Book, Art 278, and multiple travel and trade publications.

She loves to create and explore with her daughter and enjoys seeking out creative and educational experiences.

She can be contacted through her website www.KrakenSky.com and her books are available on Amazon.com

All rights reserved www.KrakenSky.com

IUCN (International Union for Conservation of Nature) Red List.
Established in 1964, the International Union for Conservation of Nature's Red List of Threatened Species has evolved to become the world's most comprehensive information source on the global extinction risk status of animal, fungus and plant species.
www.iucnredlist.org

Cornell Lab/ All About Birds
www.birds.cornell.edu

Merlin Bird ID
Free global bird guide app with photos,
sounds, maps, and more.
https://merlin.allaboutbirds.org

National Invasive Species Information Center
Identification and reporting resources from agencies and organizations with an interest in the prevention, control, or eradication of invasive species.
www.invasivespeciesinfo.gov

CitizenScience.gov
CitizenScience.gov's mission is to nurture collaboration between the federal government and the public to advance inclusive participation in scientific discovery and research.
www.citizenscience.gov/

Citizen Science Projects NASA
Join NASA researchers and discover the secrets of the universe, search for life elsewhere, and protect, and improve life on Earth and in space.
https://science.nasa.gov/citizen-science

Florida Fish and Wildlife Conservation Commission
Managing fish and wildlife resources for their long-term well-being and the benefit of people.
https://myfwc.com

National Park Service
www.nps.gov

Geocaching
Information and app download
www.geocaching.com

Please let me know if you see any printing or fact errors, so I may update accordingly! Also, check out my downloadable resource list and contact information here:
https://linktr.ee/KrakenSky

All rights reserved www.KrakenSky.com

Made in United States
Orlando, FL
05 January 2025